Book 2   Oxford Social Geographies

Martin Simons   **Three Giant Powers**

Studies in   Russia
the Union of Soviet Socialist Republics
China
the People's Republic of China
America
the United States of America

Oxford University Press

Oxford University Press, Walton Street, Oxford OX2 6DP
OXFORD LONDON GLASGOW
NEW YORK TORONTO MELBOURNE WELLINGTON
NAIROBI DAR ES SALAAM CAPE TOWN
KUALA LUMPUR SINGAPORE JAKARTA HONG KONG TOKYO
DELHI BOMBAY CALCUTTA MADRAS KARACHI

© Oxford University Press 1974

First published 1974
Reprinted 1976, 1978, and 1979

Acknowledgements

The author and publishers gratefully acknowledge permission to use the following copyright material:

From G. Jorré, *Soviet Union*, by permission of Longman Group Ltd., Fig. 2a; from G. T. Trewartha, *Introduction to Climate*, © 1968 by McGraw-Hill Book Company and used with their permission and from G. R. Rumney, *Climatology and World Climates*, © 1968 by Macmillan Publishing Co. Inc. of New York and used with their permission, 7; from G. J. Demko, Rose & Schnell, *Population Geography*, © 1970 by McGraw-Hill Book Company and used with their permission, 17; from *Geography*, 51, 380 by permission of The Geographical Association, 19; from K. Buchanan, *Transformation of the Chinese Earth*, by permission of G. Bell & Sons Ltd., 20, 29; from A. L. Rodgers, *International Geographical Union Proceedings*, 1952, Congress, by permission of the editor, 22; from J. S. Gregory, *Russian Land and Soviet People*, © 1968 Bobbs-Merrill and used with their permission, 23; from R. S. Thoman and D. J. Patton (ed.), *Focus on Geographic Activity*, © 1964 by McGraw-Hill Book Company and used with their permission, 25, 33, 37, 43; from A. B. A. Hutson, *Sample Studies Round the World*, by permission of Mills & Boon, 26; from J. P. Cole, *Pelican Geography of USSR*, by permission of Penguin Books, 36; from *Man's Domain: A Thematic Atlas of the World*, 2nd. ed. © 1970 by General Drafting Co. and used with their permission, 38; from C. L. White *et al*, *Regional Geography of Anglo-America* 4th ed. © 1974 Prentice-Hall, Inc. and used with their permission, 40; from *China in Maps*, ed. H. Fullard by permission of George Philip & Son Ltd., 46a; from *Geographical Review*, July 1965, © 1965 by the American Geographical Society and used with their permission, 48; from *Focus*, 1966, © 1966 by the American Geographical Society and used with their permission, 48; from W. Miller, *Leningrad*, by permission of J. M. Dent & Sons Ltd., 50.

Eve Arnold (Magnum), Photo 84; Bruno Barbey (Magnum), 158; Brian Brake (Magnum), 9; Camera Press, 10, 12, 13, 16, 17, 22, 31, 39, 40, 49, 56–60, 68–70, 72–3, 78, 82, 90, 103, 105, 114, 117, 118, 120, 121, 131, 134, 136, 137, 141, 151, 155, 157, 161, 163; Henri Cartier-Bresson (Magnum), 8, 18, 20, 25, 50, 51, 65, 71, 94, 140, 170; J. Allan Cash, 26, 34–36, 45, 46, 64, 75–77, 80, 110, 119, 133, 138, 143–146, 149, 150, 153, 156, 164, 165, 177; Cornell Capa (Magnum), 147; Martin J. Dain (Magnum), 24, 112; Elliott Erwitt (Magnum), 129; Exxon Corporation, 124; Leonard Freed (Magnum), 28, 81; Georg Gerster (Magnum), 52, 154; Richard and Sally Greenhill, 3, 4, 42, 66, 91, 92, 97, 167, 176; R. C. Hunt, 30; Keystone Press Agency, 32, 61, 85, 93, 107; Lee Wilson and Co., 111; Magnum, 1, 14, 41, 86, 122, 139, 173; Mansell Collection, 96, 98, 99–102, 104; John Massey Stewart, 89, 162, 174; James Mitchell (Magnum), 83, 152; Novosti Press Agency, 2, 5, 19, 29, 33, 37, 38, 44, 47, 48, 53, 62, 74, 79, 88, 108, 113, 115, 116, 123, 126, 128, 130, 142, 148, 166, 169, 172, 175; Marc Riboud (Magnum), 55, 95, 106, 168; Ted Spiegel (Magnum), 109; United States Information Service, 7, 11, 21, 54, 63, 87, 127; United Press International, 6, 15, 23, 27, 43, 67, 159, 160.

Newspaper headlines, p.7 from the *Daily Mail*, *Evening Standard*, *The Guardian*, *The Times*.

Filmset by BAS Printers Limited, Over Wallop, Hampshire
and printed in Great Britain at the University Press, Oxford
by Eric Buckley, Printer to the University

Contents

	Preface	4
	Introduction	7
1	Recognizing the Giants	12
2	Communism and Capitalism	18
3	Controlling the Giants	37
4	Variety of Land and Climate	40
5	Variety of Peoples	54
6	Farming Communities	69
7	Industries	88
8	Growing Cities	111
9	Satellites and Allies	132
	The Future . . .	138
	Index	144

Photo. 1 American high school students cheer their football team
Photo. 2 A children's library in Moscow

Preface

Anyone who attempts a comparative study of the three great powers, China, the U.S.S.R., and the United States, even at an elementary level, runs the risk of being wrong about all three. In the case of the U.S.A., so much information is available that any selection made must to some extent be arbitrary. As a result, the emphasis on any aspect of a controversial issue must depend to a large extent on the facts singled out for study. Even then, when the study is made, the U.S.A. is changing so rapidly that the most well-known and accepted generalizations can soon become myths.

In the case of the U.S.S.R., rapid changes and developments are no less obvious, but to assess their impact and to spot trends is harder than in the case of the U.S.A., since information is often lacking. While information emanating from the central government is now much more voluminous than it once was, it must be recognized that it is as a rule information which the government chooses to release. There are no independent sources, other than the few travellers and scholars who have been able to observe the country at first hand, in a necessarily personalized and localized manner.

In China the same remarks apply with even more force, and in addition it is at times obvious that the Chinese government itself does not have reliable data even for its own purposes. The statistics are not falsified; in most cases there simply are no statistics at all. The population is so vast and the regional differences in development are so great that there is often no common basis upon which a rational structure of central planning could be erected. In such a context, the development of communes and the recent emphasis on decentralization of industry, and with it, the partial transference of some planning powers to local and regional authorities, makes a great deal of sense but adds further difficulties for the outside observer. Over and above all this lies the shadow of Mao Tse-tung, the Cultural Revolution, and the prospect of further political changes since Mao's death. Perhaps the only reasonably safe statement is that not even a revolutionary war followed by nearly 30 years of communist rule, including a cultural revolution, has fully awakened the sleeping giant, China. When the full awakening does take place, Peking may be the first to hear of it, but neither Peking nor anyone else can predict the consequences.

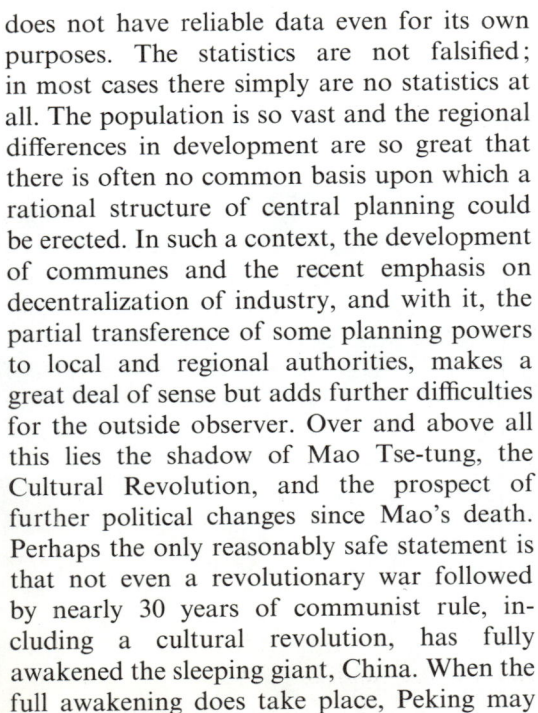

Faced with such difficulties, very few authors of school books have dared to attempt the kind of simplification that has been attempted here. Yet, it seems, someone has to rush in. The three giants must not be ignored by the schools, for they are not fairy-tale giants. It is hoped that this book will help to clear away some of the myths which surround all three, and if any new myths seem to be established by it, the author must accept full responsibility.

Photo. 3 A Chinese woman prepares a meal for her family

Photo 4 Learning to do arithmetic on the abacus in a Chinese school

Photo. 5   Chinese soldiers attacking Soviet troop positions on the frontier in 1969

Photo. 6   A North Vietnamese girl holds an American Air Force pilot at the point of her rifle. The Vietnam War (see p. 135) was a struggle between powers, China supporting the North and the U.S.A. the South

Photo. 7   Missile sites equipped by the U.S.S.R. in Cuba in 1962. At this time Russia and the United States seemed very close to war

Introduction

This book is about the three great powers. Each is described by a number of names:

Geographical	Official	Initials	Popular name
China	The People's Republic of China		Red China
America	United States of America	USA	The States
The Soviet Union	The Union of Soviet Socialist Republics	USSR	Russia

These three giant powers are often in the news. Whenever something happens that affects them, everyone in the world seems to take special notice. What is more, each of the three seems very concerned about the other two. Some news stories suggest that they are constantly arguing with one another, and at other times there are trade agreements and conferences, with talk of co-existence and an end to the 'cold war'.

In the Second World War, which ended in 1945, the U.S.A., China, and the U.S.S.R. were **allies** against Germany and Japan. Within a few years, however, quarrels broke out, particularly at first between the Soviet Union and the U.S.A. When China, too, began to play a greater part in world affairs, she came into conflict first with the U.S.A. and, later, with the U.S.S.R. also. The photographs and cuttings illustrate some of the 'incidents' that have occurred during the past 20 years. All three powers have very large armed forces; if ever a full-scale war did break out between the three, or between any two of them, it would certainly affect every person in the world and such a war could bring about the end of civilized life.

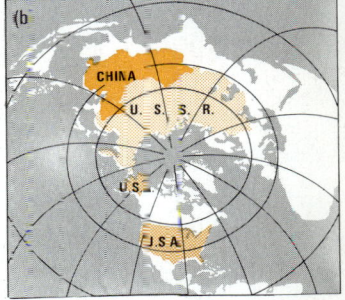

Fig. 1 (a) The world drawn to compare the areas of China, U.S.A., and the U.S.S.R.; (b) North polar projection showing the proximity of the three powers

7

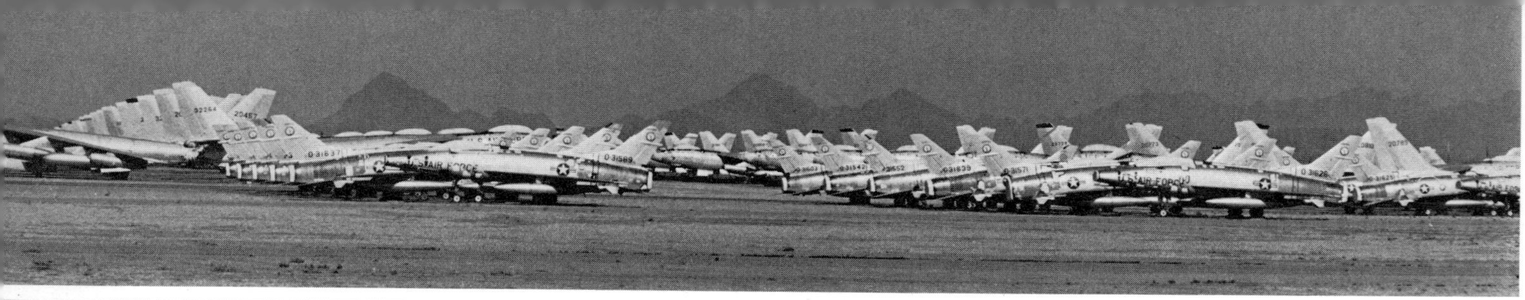

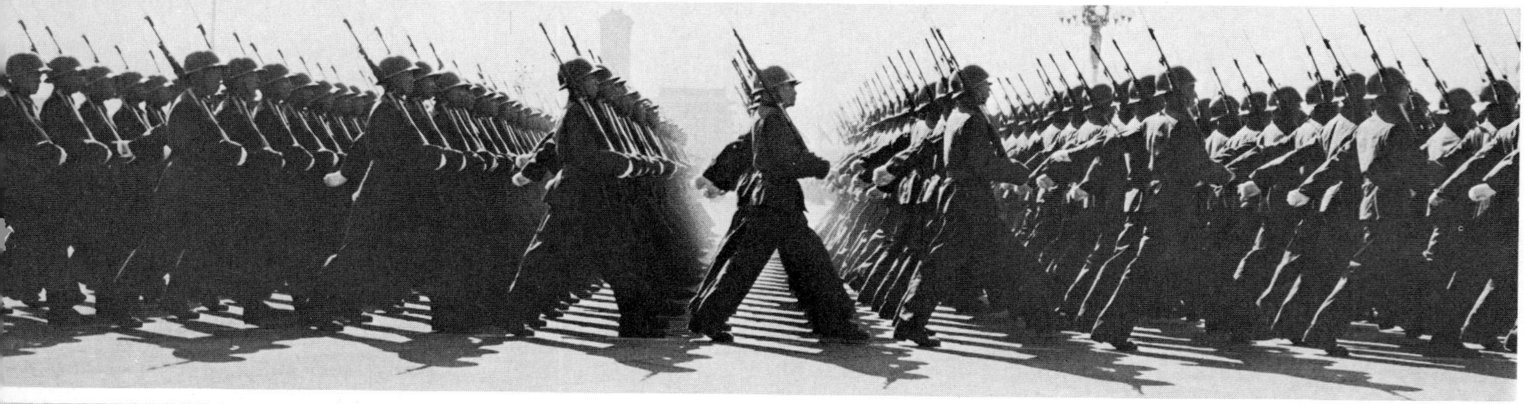

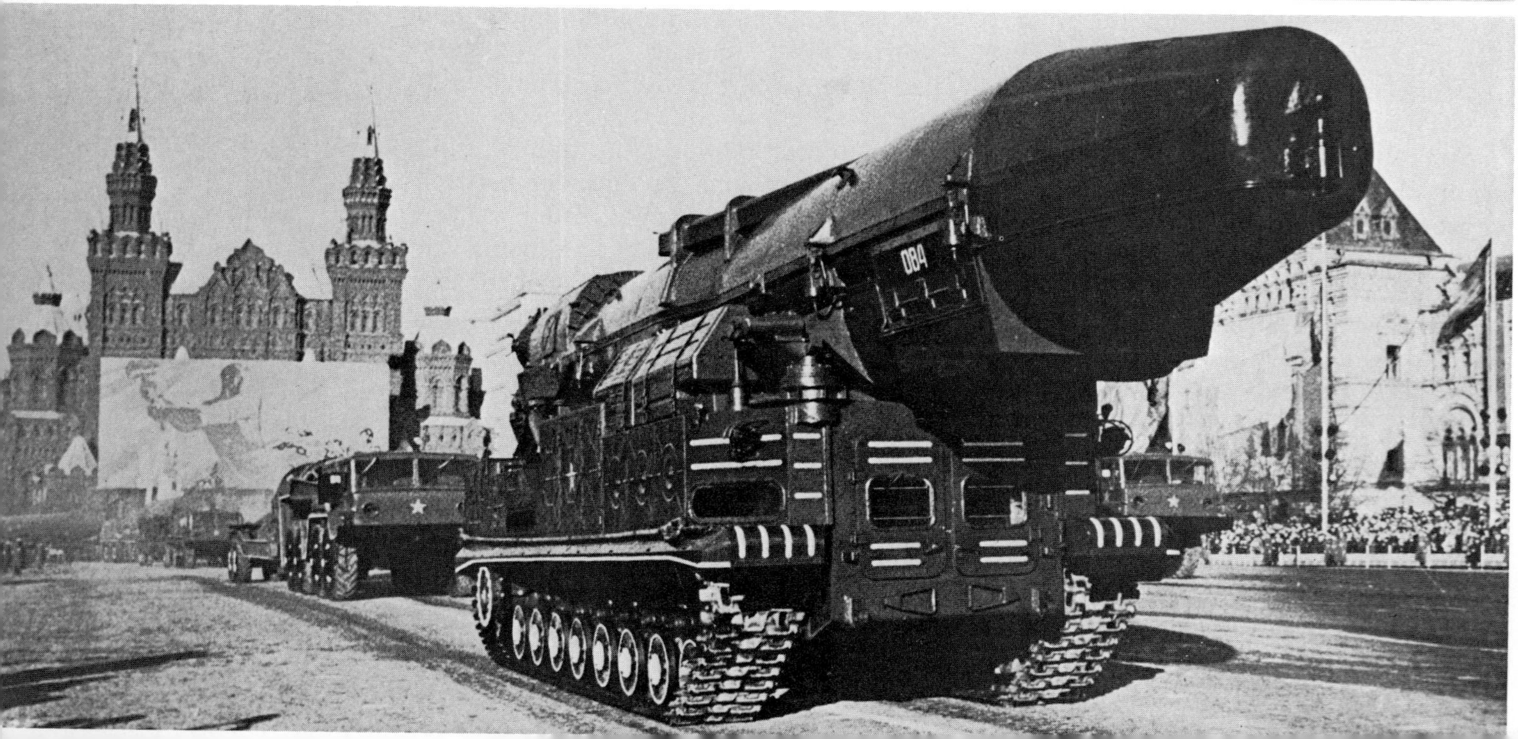
084

One reason why all three giants put so much effort into building up and maintaining their military power is simply that they are afraid of one another. Each power fears that there may be an attack by the others, and they struggle to make themselves so strong that any such attack could be beaten off. The U.S.A. and the U.S.S.R. have both launched 'spy satellites' into orbit around the earth. These pass over the rival countries and transmit pictures of the ground which show any secret military work, such as the building of new missile bases and armament factories. As soon as one of the giant powers develops a new weapon, the other two rush to achieve the same strength. This has led to an arms race which still goes on, even when the arguments die down for a time. For example, the U.S.A. exploded the first hydrogen bomb in 1952, the U.S.S.R. followed with an H-bomb in 1953, and in 1968 China announced that she, too, had the H-bomb. Yet such a weapon is nothing to be proud of. It can be used only for destruction. One such bomb delivered by rocket missile would almost completely destroy a city the size of London, and deadly radiation from the explosion could continue killing people in the rest of Britain for months or years afterwards.

Photo. 11 Explosion of a nuclear weapon, in this case a test by the U.S.A.

Opposite page, from the top:

Photo. 8 Line-up of U.S. Air Force military aircraft

Photo. 9 May Day parade of armed forces in Peking

Photo. 10 Military power on show in the U.S.S.R. A huge rocket missile moves through Red Square in Moscow

Photo. 12 Part of the U.S. space programme. The commander of the Apollo 17 mission checks the Lunar Roving Vehicle

Photo. 13 A Soviet cosmonaut 'swims' in space

Other sorts of competition between the giants have also been going on for some time. The U.S.A. and the U.S.S.R. both have programmes of space exploration; great rockets have been used to launch space probes. The U.S.A. was first to land men on the moon, but a U.S.S.R. robot vehicle came soon after, and the Russians have completed some parts of their space programme before the Americans. China's first space satellite was launched in 1971, indicating that they are making efforts to catch up with the other two.

Yet while the tension remains and flares up again from time to time, there are signs that the three giant powers are gradually working out ways of existing together, and even co-operating. In 1972 the U.S.A. and U.S.S.R. agreed to limit development of some very expensive defence systems, and there were trade agreements between these two powers. In the same year President Nixon of the U.S.A. visited China and met Chinese leaders, Mao Tse-tung and Chou En-lai. The U.S.A., after refusing for more than twenty years, finally agreed that 'Red China' should be allowed to join the United Nations.

There are, and always have been, many important differences between the three giant powers, yet they are also very alike in other ways and as time goes on they may be growing more alike. In this book an attempt is made to compare them.

Assignments

1. Make a scrapbook of newspaper and magazine articles and pictures dealing with the three great powers. Pay special attention to statements made by the leaders of each nation about the other two.

2. Discuss with your friends and teacher the reasons why some countries become enemies.

Photo. 14 President Nixon of the U.S.A. meets Chairman Mao in 1972

Photo. 15 President Nixon (seated left) and Russian leader Leonid Brezhnev (standing behind seats) signing an agreement to limit their countries' production of armaments. This photograph was taken in the Vladimir Hall at the Kremlin

11

1 Recognizing the Giants

Size

The world map (Fig. 1a) has been drawn to show correctly the size of land and sea areas. Some maps make countries appear too large or small; only a globe will show everything correct in both area and shape. The six largest countries in the world are listed in Table 1.

Table 1

Name of country	Approximate area in km²
U.S.S.R.	22 400 000
Canada	10 000 000
China	9 700 000
U.S.A.	9 300 000
Brazil	8 500 000
Australia	7 700 000

Canada is actually larger in area than China or the U.S.A.; Brazil and Australia are not very much smaller. They, too, are giants in land area, but cannot be called giant *powers*. Canada's huge land area is for the most part almost empty and the total population of the country is far less than that of some small area nations such as Japan and Britain.

Opposite page:

Photo. 16 Crowds gather for the May Day procession in Red Square, Moscow

Photo. 17 Crowds of people on the beach at Coney Island, New York, U.S.A.

Photo. 18 As many as 50 000 people at a time helped in the construction of the Ming Tombs Dam near Peking in China

Population

One source of a great power's strength is in people. Table 2 gives the six largest countries in terms of their total population.

Table 2

Name of country	Population (approx., see note)
China	700 000 000
India	509 000 000
U.S.S.R.	239 000 000
U.S.A.	203 000 000
Indonesia	118 000 000
Japan	103 000 000

Note: To measure the population of any large country is very difficult, since even while the census is being taken, people die, babies are born, and some emigrate or arrive as immigrants. The figures in the table are rough estimates. The true population of China is not known even by the Chinese government. Recent estimates have varied from 700 to over 800 million. The last official census was in 1953, the number then being 583 million. In 1971 Li Hsien-nien, the Chinese Vice Premier, admitted that ministries quote figures as different as 750 and 830 million. It is calculated that a quarter of the world's population lives in China. Many millions more Chinese live abroad in South-East Asia and in America.

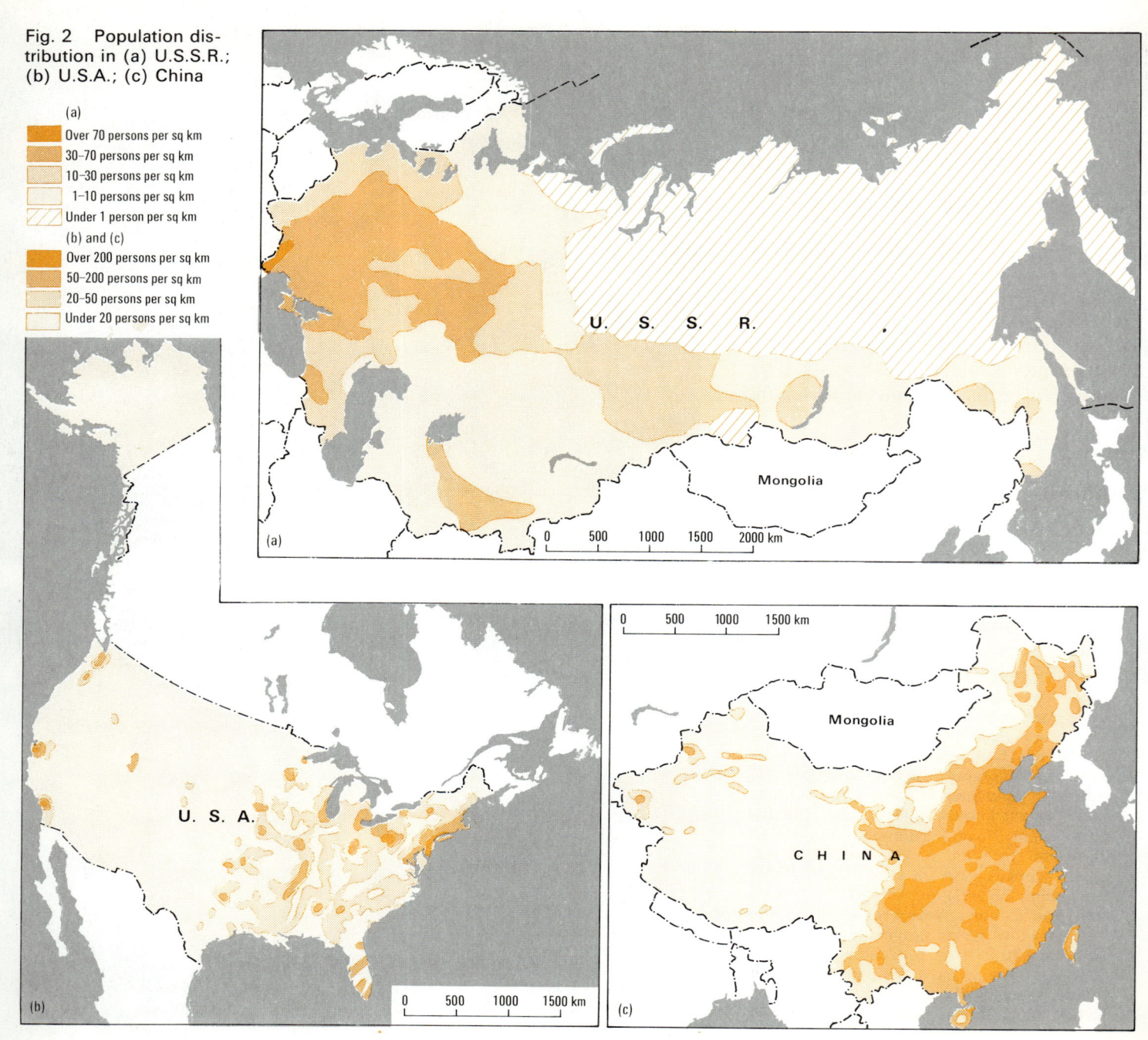

Fig. 2 Population distribution in (a) U.S.S.R.; (b) U.S.A.; (c) China

(a)
- Over 70 persons per sq km
- 30–70 persons per sq km
- 10–30 persons per sq km
- 1–10 persons per sq km
- Under 1 person per sq km

(b) and (c)
- Over 200 persons per sq km
- 50–200 persons per sq km
- 20–50 persons per sq km
- Under 20 persons per sq km

Wealth

The U.S.A. has a smaller population than China, and is smaller in area than the U.S.S.R., but in wealth and industrial strength it is the most powerful giant of all. Table 3 gives the production figures for three of the most important commodities; steel, oil and electric power. You will read more about industry in Chapter 7.

Population and production figures can sometimes change very rapidly. The U.S.S.R. is making great efforts to increase industrial production and hopes to equal or surpass the U.S.A. before many years have passed. China is far less industrialized than the other powers, but also has plans to step up growth. The population in all three countries is growing, but most rapidly in China, which is already by far the biggest.

Photo. 19 The great Dnieper Dam in the Ukraine, U.S.S.R., provides electric power for many major industries
Photo. 20 A modern power station in China contrasts with the crude cart used for transport
Photo. 21 Industrial plant at Kingsport, Tennessee, U.S.A.

Table 3

	Production Figures (per year)		
	U.S.A.	U.S.S.R.	China
Crude steel (tonnes)	119 260 000	106 538 000	23 000 000
Crude oil (millions of barrels)	3042·000	1918·000	200·00
Electric power (millions of kilowatt hours)	1 435 522	638 661	60 000

Note: One kilowatt hour is a sufficient quantity of electricity to keep a small electric radiator burning for one hour.

Fig. 3 Area graphs. One small square represents 100 000 km², so the U.S.S.R. is represented by 224 squares, arranged in a column 10 squares wide and 22·4 squares high

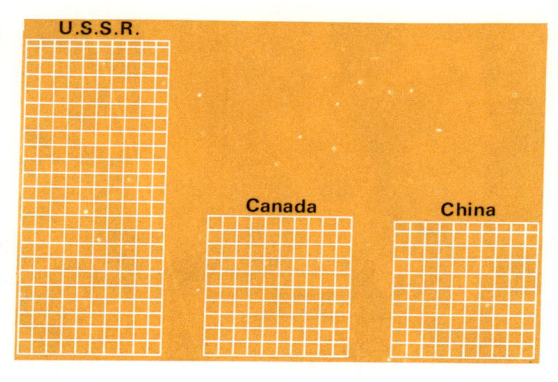

Assignments

1. Study the photographs in this book and note the points of difference and similarity between the powers.

2. (a) Using a globe, and a piece of string, measure and compare the distances between the places listed below:
New York (U.S.A.) to San Francisco (U.S.A.)
Shanghai (China) to Kashgar (China)
Hong Kong to Peking (China)
Moscow (U.S.S.R.) to Vladivostock (U.S.S.R.)
Tashkent (U.S.S.R.) to Vorkuta (U.S.S.R.)
(b) Suppose you were flying an aeroplane at 800 km per hour, how long would each of these journeys take, and over which parts of the globe might you fly?
Peking (China) to Washington (U.S.A.)
Washington (U.S.A.) to Moscow (U.S.S.R.)
Los Angeles (U.S.A.) to Moscow (U.S.S.R.)
Canton (China) to Chicago (U.S.A.)
Peking (China) to Moscow (U.S.S.R.)
Some of these flights involve flying across countries which might forbid it, for political reasons. Air-liners do not always follow the shortest routes.

3. (a) Draw a diagram illustrating differences in land area between the three countries; use squared paper as shown in Fig. 3.

Population Density

The total population of a country, divided by the total land area, gives a figure called the average **population density** for that country. For example, China's population density is
700 000 000 ÷ 9 700 000 =
72·1 people per square kilometre.
This means that for each square kilometre (km²) of land there are about 72 or 73 people in China.

The population density for U.S.A. is worked out in the same way:
203 000 000 ÷ 9 300 000 = 21·8 people/km²
a much lower density than the Chinese figure. In the Soviet Union the density of population averages just over 10/km². In Chapter 4, however, these figures are examined again, and are shown to give a somewhat oversimplified impression.

Take one small square to represent 100 000 square kilometres, then from the table of the areas (Table 1, p. 12), the land area of the U.S.S.R. will be represented by a column 10 squares wide and 22·4 high. Canada will be shown by a column 10 by 10, China 10 by 9·7, and so on.

Find out from a reference book or encyclopaedia the areas of other countries, both large and small, and add to this diagram.

(b) Draw a diagram to compare populations, using squared paper. Take each small square to represent one million people. The population of China can then be represented by a block measuring 20 squares along the base and standing 35 squares high. India would then be represented by a block 20 squares on the base by 25·4 high. The other figures may be worked out in similar fashion, and the populations of some other countries, obtained from a reference book, may be shown in this way and added to the diagram.

(c) Production figures may be represented on squared paper in a similar way to population and area. Use one small square to represent one million tonnes of steel, or one million barrels of oil, or 100 000 kilowatt hours of electric power.

4. The population and production figures in this chapter will have changed since this book was published. You can check these figures, and find others to compare them with in any newly-published atlas or encyclopaedia, or in the most recent *Whitaker's Almanack*. The local library will have them and possibly the school library. *Whitaker's Almanack* is published every year with revised figures for population and production, and much other information.

Photo. 22 A review march of young people in Tien Anmen Square in Peking. The Tien Anmen Gate is on the right of the picture, the old 'Forbidden City' (see p. 116) is behind it

Photo. 23 Balloons, flags, and excitement: the atmosphere of an American political convention. In this picture the Republican Party have just chosen Richard Nixon as their candidate for the Presidential election

2 Communism and Capitalism

There are fundamental differences in the ways the governments of the great powers are chosen. The U.S.S.R. and China are governed by their **communist** parties. The people have no opportunity to vote for any opposition party for these are illegal. The U.S.A. considers itself to be a **democratic** country. When elections are held for the Presidency and for Members of Congress, every adult can choose to vote for a candidate; the candidate represents any one of a number of parties. The two major ones are the Republicans and Democrats.

The economic system, the organization of work and production, is also very different. In a socialist or communist state, land, factories, railways—all the means of production, and most property—belong to the people. The state represents the people. Every person works and in return for his work receives enough pay—usually in money, but sometimes in foodstuffs—for his basic needs. Food and rents are cheap. Wages are kept fairly level. Senior officials and professional men and women are paid more than labourers, but the difference between the lowest and highest salary is not too great.

In the U.S.A., both the Republican and Democratic parties support a free **capitalist** system of distributing wealth. Wages and salaries are more unequal than in socialist countries, but the biggest difference is in the laws of property. An individual may own his house, and also land, a factory, or shares in a factory and he has the right to pass this capital on to his children when he dies. A man may invest money in land or in shares of a business and this **capital** may grow in value. Some families are very much richer than others because they have inherited the wealth made by parents and grandparents. Despite the income spread in the U.S.A., the great bulk of the population have greater material wealth than the people of China and the U.S.S.R., because the U.S. living standard is very high in general.

Photo. 24   An extreme example of the uneven distribution of capitalist wealth: a negro cotton-picking family in Mississippi, U.S.A. Only a small proportion of American people are as poor as this

Photo. 25   An electrical works in China. The factory belongs to the state

Photo. 26   Privately-owned boats, Florida, U.S.A.

Photo. 27 A Senate Committee hears evidence on 'the Watergate affair'. A public inquiry, complete with pressmen and television cameras, was called in 1973 to investigate allegations of corruption in the U.S. government. This process is possible only in a democratic country

Freedom of the individual

There is a small Communist Party in the U.S.A. but the government there is strongly against it, and at one time, during the early 1950s, many of the communist leaders in the States served short prison sentences.

In China and the U.S.S.R. capitalism is often regarded as a crime. In the U.S.S.R., some writers who have criticized the government, even in novels, are in prison because of their political views.

Perhaps the biggest difference between the two systems is in the personal freedom allowed to the individual. In a capitalist state, anyone can own a newspaper or television network, and anyone can write a book. There is no shortage of information or news; criticism of the government is continuous. Court trials and law cases are open to the public, and fully reported. It is possible, and quite common, for people to hire lawyers and to take a branch of the government to court if it has acted illegally. The law courts are independent of government and politics.

In communist countries the state is directly in control of all the big factories,

Five Year Plans

After the revolution in the U.S.S.R., the communist government realized that drastic action would be needed to change the whole life of the country and bring it rapidly up to date. Most of the people before had been peasants working the land, but a modern state must, the leaders thought, have great industries, and the peasant farmers would have to change their ways. In 1928, ten years after the revolution, the first 'five year plan' was announced. Targets were set for increased production and greater efficiency in farming, factories, and offices. At the same time many new industries were to be built, sometimes far away from the old centres, in the Ural Mountains, for example. The whole great scheme for modernization and expansion was to be pushed through in five years, no one was allowed to stand in the way. Anyone who did object was forced to work for the plan as a labourer in a prison camp. The peasants, who although very poor, did have their own small farms (often rented from a wealthy landlord), were forced into collective farms, and were made to hand over their crops to the government. Development costs money, and there was little available, so the people had to give up what they had, their lands, their crops, and their freedom. Richer farmers were killed.

By means of propaganda, exciting wall posters, films, and speeches from communist leaders, the Soviet people, especially in the cities, were persuaded to work for the plan, and to the world's astonishment, most of the targets were reached within four years, even more rapidly than expected. The main aims, providing more electric power and basic industry, were accomplished. Although there was terrible hardship, hunger, and poverty throughout the land, the new industrial Russia was born, and high standards of production were established.

Another five year plan was launched in the U.S.S.R. in 1933, concentrating on iron and steel plants, and railways, and a third plan was interrupted by the Second World War. Since then the U.S.S.R. has launched new five year plans at intervals, and although some have succeeded, others have been disappointing.

In China, following the U.S.S.R.'s example, a five year plan was announced in 1953 and ended in 1957. It was a great success; both food output and industrial production increased very rapidly. A second plan was started in 1958 and at first went very well, but a severe drought struck the communes in 1959, 1960, and 1961, and food production fell. In industry, mistakes were made in planning, and many small, very inefficient steel plants were started which produced large amounts of poor-quality, useless steel while the workers who were wasting their time and energy on this could have been helping in the fields of their communes, or doing other more productive work. Having recovered from this, a further five year plan followed in 1966 but it too was interrupted, this time by the so-called Cultural Revolution. (See p. 24)

businesses, airlines, railways, schools, farms, and banks. Plans are made and the government makes as sure as possible that these are pushed through, however many people may disagree. When the plans are good, this may work well, but if the planners err the country suffers. Professional men, doctors, teachers, and lawyers are paid by the state; newspapers and books are all published by the government; there

Photo. 28 A demonstration in Washington against government policy. Personal freedom of this kind is unknown in China and the U.S.S.R.

is no independent television or radio, and hardly any advertising. People thus can read, or see, only what the government approves of. Serious criticisms are rarely published. Anyone who writes a book, or even speaks publicly in opposition to the government, is likely to be severely reprimanded, or even imprisoned.

In a communist state, people may be directed by the government to move to another area to work and live, in order to carry out some vital part of a great plan. The good of the country is considered more important than the happiness or comfort of any individual person.

Supporters of communism believe that it is an advantage to share wealth more evenly. No one becomes very rich at the expense of others, and there is no serious poverty unless for some reason the whole country is poor. The government tends to look after people who are ill or who have had bad luck, but everyone who can do so is required to work. Capitalism leaves more freedom of choice to the individual. He can become as rich as he likes *if* he can make his business successful. But there is competition between businesses and between people. When one man becomes rich, others may fail in business and become poor. This may be a matter of skill or enterprise, but it is also sometimes a matter of luck or accident. A man might become ill and lose his job or fail to keep his business going. At the very same time he may have medical bills to pay which will take any money he has left. In the U.S.A. there is a 'medicare' system for the elderly but no national health service is provided by the government, so sick people often become poor very quickly. Private insurance schemes do not cover everyone's needs for medical care.

When there is profit to be made, there is temptation to be dishonest or to trick people. People who are very poor may decide to steal from the rich they see all around them, or from the company they work for. Capitalism, or the inequalities of wealth it produces, has thus been blamed for turning some people into criminals. But there is crime in communist countries too; workers there are sometimes searched as they leave their factories, and government officials can be tempted to take bribes from people wanting special favours. Communism has not solved the crime problem either.

Photo. 29 A meeting held in Moscow in 1970 to celebrate Lenin's centenary. Lenin was born in 1870, and died in 1924. His tomb in Moscow can be seen in Photo. 137

History

In Russia and China communist governments took power after great revolutions and civil wars. At the beginning of this century both these vast countries were ruled by emperors, and their chosen advisers. The vast majority of Russians and Chinese were peasants.

Russia

The Russian peasants had been serfs for hundreds of years. They were forced to work the land belonging to the nobles. Even after they were freed, and that was not until 1861 (compare the date with the abolition of slavery in America), they had very little land to farm, and usually the poorest soil. The nobles and upper classes owned the best land, and all the factories, mills, shipping, and other assets.

There were strikes, riots, and revolts by the town workers in the early years of this century, and a major revolution broke out in 1917. There were a lot of different ideas on how to reform the government, and the Bolsheviks, the branch of the Communist Party that took power in the cities, was not the biggest party. Under the leadership of Lenin, the communists fought a civil war, and established a government. The Russian people suffered a great deal while the state took over factories, railways, and finally the land. Wealthy landowners and peasants lost all they had, many of them were killed, and all over the country, people experienced the hardship and misery of civil war.

Photo. 30 Red Guards at a rally in Peking hold up their little red books, *The Thoughts of Mao Tse-tung*. Notice these little books lying on each desk in Photo. 4

The death of Mao in 1976 is likely to have a big effect on China's future. Perhaps his thoughts will not seem so important to young people who cannot remember when he was alive.

Photo. 31 This poster of Mao was used to introduce the Cultural Revolution on 5 August 1966

The Cultural Revolution

In 1965 Mao Tse-tung, the Chairman of the Chinese Communist Party and the most important leader in the country, felt that many of his colleagues in the government were not pushing forward fast enough with communist reforms; they were tending to lose sight of the ideals that guided them in the Revolution. In many places capitalist practices were still going on and not enough was being done, Mao thought, to convert the Chinese peasants, many of whom had no interest in communism and no enthusiasm for change. Mao therefore called on the young students in schools and universities, and on the Chinese army, to help him bring about what he called a Cultural Revolution. It was not enough merely to have the communists in power, the whole way of thought of the nation had to be changed.

The Red Guards, mainly students in their teens and early twenties, formed bands, demonstrated in the streets, and launched critical, sometimes violent, attacks on the older party officials and on anyone who, to

China

China in the early years of this century was poor, and weakly governed. Peasants worked on land that belonged to rich landowners who often lived in the cities. Rents and taxes were high and many villagers were in debt all their lives.

As in Russia there were various ideas on how to reform the country. The Communist Party was founded in 1921, and Mao Tse-tung, a member from the beginning, fought for 28 years for a communist revolution. Above all things he believed that the people should own the land they worked on. He established

them, seemed to be standing in the way of progress towards the pure communist state. The army stood behind Mao and enforced his wishes; many of the men who had been with him in the government were sacked and replaced by those who favoured Mao's leadership, and for about two years the whole country was full of disturbances. Schools and colleges were often closed as the Red Guards carried out their campaigns. They were helped by Mao himself to make up posters calling for the bombardment of the Communist Party headquarters where, it was thought, the enemies of the Revolution were to be found.

The peasants, and the industrial workers, however, resisted the Red Guards and there were many clashes between the workers and the students. Often the younger Communist Party men used the Cultural Revolution as an excuse to get rid of the senior officials in their towns and villages, so that they could take over. In many cases the result was chaos. Families were sometimes broken up when the children joined the Red Guards and attacked their parents because they were not enthusiastic communists. Peasant farmers lost the right in many places to farm their own gardens.

In the high ranks of the Communist Party even Liu Shao-chi, who had been Mao's deputy, was strongly criticized, publicly insulted, and deposed. In 1966 Liu was replaced as Mao's deputy by Lin Piao, an army general who had risen to become China's defence minister. However, although Lin Piao joined Mao's side in the Cultural Revolution period, it was announced in 1972 that during the previous year he had attempted to assassinate Mao and to take over his power. Lin had failed and tried to escape to the U.S.S.R., but he was killed when the aeroplane he was using for the escape crashed. The Cultural Revolution finally collapsed because of its excesses, the army often stepping in to help the peasants and workers to regain control from the Red Guards. The effects of the Cultural Revolution on the future of China are very hard to assess. For a time it strengthened Mao Tse-tung's personal control of the nation. Now that he is dead the power structure has changed.

Photo. 32 These young girls of the Hsia-an brigade in Fukien province take part in bayonet training. Workers and students from every part of the country are encouraged to form military units.

a soviet government in the south, and then when driven out, marched 9600 kilometres—the Long March—with his followers to Yenan in the north. There he founded another soviet (see p. 38). The war against Japan interrupted the civil war, and it was not until 1949 that Mao established the People's Republic of China over the whole country.

The first major task was to get rid of the landowners, and turn the land over to co-operative farming. Mao personally directed the modern development of China, and all over the country people looked to him for inspiration and guidance.

Photo. 34 Mt. Vernon, home of George Washington who led the rebellion against British rule, and became first president of the U.S.A.

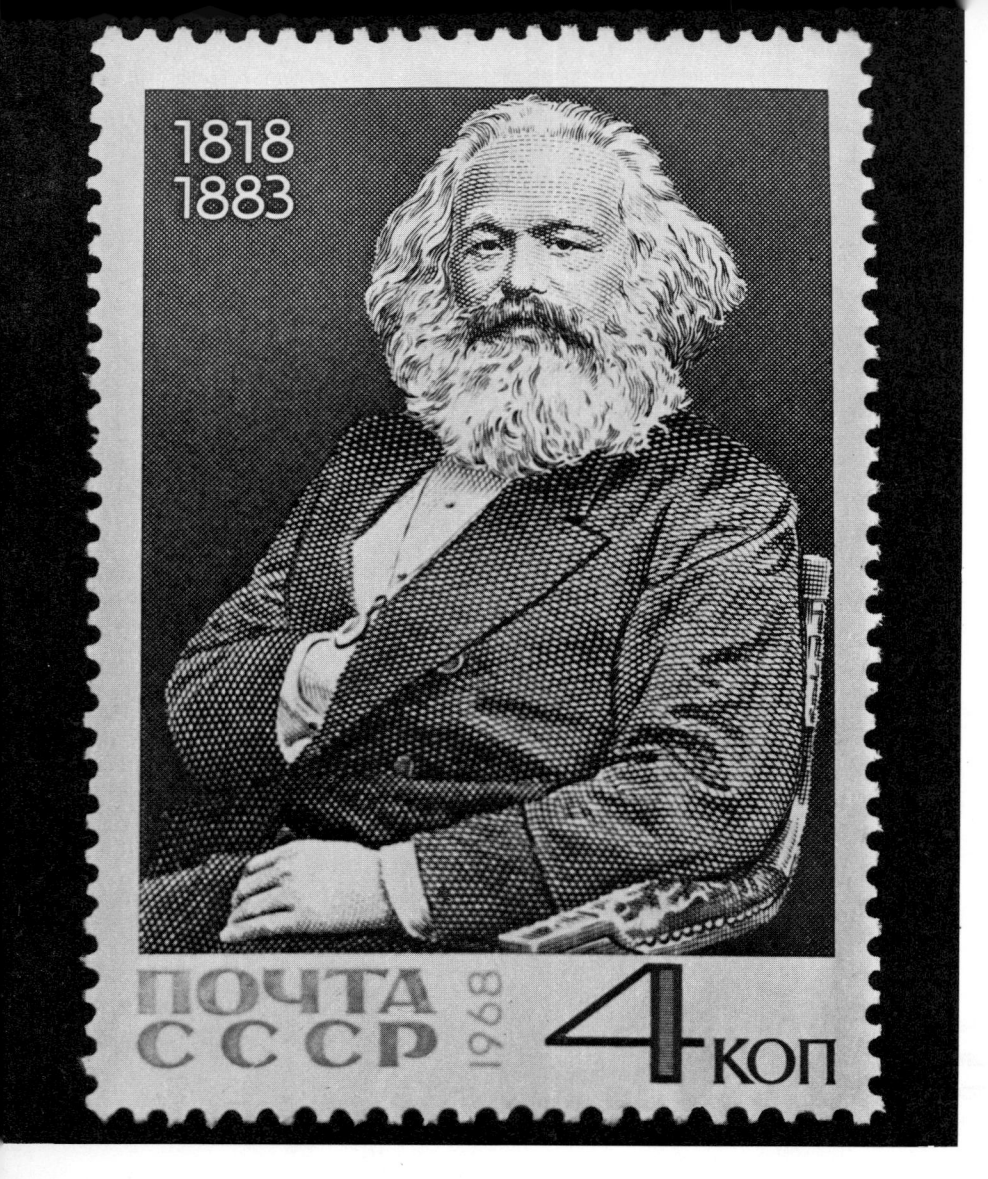

Photo. 33 Karl Marx, the founder of communism, portrayed on a Soviet stamp

Karl Marx

Lenin and Mao followed the teaching of Karl Marx, whose great book, *Capital*, blamed the capitalist system, rather than the particular rulers or landowners, for all injustice and poverty. Karl Marx was born in 1818 and read, as a young man, about the American Revolution and the French Revolution of 1789. He saw that in spite of the upheaval, much poverty and misery still remained in those countries. Changing the rulers did not seem to have improved things for ordinary men. What he wanted was a complete change of the whole economic system. Such a change, he thought, could come only by revolution. Only when the people owned the land, the factories, and all the means of producing and exchanging wealth, would equality be possible.

Supporters of communism claim that the revolutions in the U.S.S.R. and China improved the condition of ordinary people, but in capitalist countries too, things have changed greatly and many of Karl Marx's arguments against capitalism do not seem so true more than a hundred years later. In this book, the terms 'communist country' and 'socialist country' mean the same thing. Both the U.S.S.R. and China describe themselves as socialist countries, and see 'communism' as the perfect state towards which they are working. Communism was the goal set by both Marx and Lenin.

United States

The U.S.A. also began as a nation with a revolutionary war, but the causes of this war were quite different from those of the civil wars waged in Russia and in China. The Americans of the 13 Atlantic seaboard colonies (the east coast) fought for the right to make their own laws independently of Great Britain. There was bitter fighting from 1775 until 1783 when the British troops withdrew. Unlike the U.S.S.R. and China, independence in America did not make a great deal of difference to the lives of ordinary people. They continued to own private property, to run their own businesses, and to allow individual citizens freedom to criticize the government. And the Europeans, especially the poor who emigrated to the U.S.A. over the next 150 years, went there to find more freedom and opportunity than they had known in their homelands. All this is true of the freemen only, and not of the black slaves. They were not freed until 1865, and their descendants have never had equal opportunity for education, jobs, homes, or political power.

Photo. 35 Like Mt. Vernon, the Lincoln Memorial is a national monument. Abraham Lincoln united the people of the northern and southern states after the American Civil War, and is honoured as one of the country's great heroes

27

Photo. 36 Buildings of central New York. These skyscrapers are privately built and privately owned for leasing and renting as offices

Property

Probably most people who read this book will live in a capitalist society. Under this system private people or companies can own land, property, and businesses, and work to make a cash profit. For example, a landlord may own a number of houses and charge rent for people to live in them. He will probably have to repair and maintain the houses in good order, and will pay rates and taxes on the property. He will charge a rent that will enable him to pay for the repairs and other costs, and also have some cash left over as profit for himself. If he owns a large number of houses in this way he might make so much profit that he can live comfortably without doing any other work. If he wishes he may have some or all of his houses pulled down and then pay for a block of flats or offices to be built on the same land. He would then expect to charge higher rents for the whole property, and in the long run make a bigger profit. However, if he charged too much rent, no one could afford to live in his houses or hire his offices, and the cash he spent on the building would be wasted. Depending on these, and other things, he might go bankrupt, or he might become very rich.

People who support the capitalist system claim that it works out best in the long run; a bad landlord who fails to keep his property in order, or who charges too much rent, will be unable to find tenants and so lose his money. The tenants are free to change house whenever they wish, and if they can find a landlord who charges less they will move to his property. If they can get enough money together, or borrow it, they could buy their own houses. Capitalists argue that this gives them freedom to choose where they live and how much they will spend on their housing.

This free enterprise system can work if there are enough houses for everyone, and jobs nearby. But sometimes a family cannot move house because there is no other available. A bad landlord may put up the rent, knowing that his tenants have no choice but to pay or be homeless. When tenants fail to pay the rent, they can be turned out (evicted).

But tenants may behave badly, as well as landlords. They may damage a house knowing that the landlord has to pay for the repairs. Or they may sub-let it to someone else, charge a higher rent, and keep the difference for themselves. In capitalist countries there are always a great many laws dealing with landlords and tenants. These rules are intended to prevent severe hardship and to guarantee fair dealing.

In many countries, Britain for instance, the local government may buy land and build houses, becoming itself a landlord. The rents charged for such 'council' houses are lower than private landlords charge, because the council does not try to make a profit. This arrangement is almost halfway between pure capitalism and pure communism. In the United States council housing of this type is very rare and is available only for the very poor.

In a communist state, almost all land and housing, and most other kinds of property too, are owned by the state itself and the government is the landlord. Tenants pay rent to the government, not to any individual person or property company. The government does not try to make a profit out of housing. It charges rents that go towards the construction and upkeep of buildings, so rents in communist countries are lower than in western capitalist countries.

There are disadvantages. The tenant has little choice. He cannot change his landlord. If he does not like the flat he is in, or feels the rent is too high, the chances are that all the flats and rents are the same. A flat may go with a job. A worker who loses his job can lose his right to live in his city flat. A man who criticizes the government may be turned out of his home. Whereas in a capitalist country he can call on the law to protect him against his landlord, in a communist country lawyers are government officials and the law does not protect the individual.

Photo. 37 Children playing in a Moscow courtyard. These apartment blocks are owned by the state and leased to tenants at very small cost

Photo. 38 This new housing estate in Leningrad is government built and government owned

29

Photo. 39 A large modern food shop in Moscow

Photo. 40 The famous state-owned department store, Gum, in Moscow. Compare this with the more modern shopping scene in Photo. 39.

Business

In a capitalist state, any person is free to start his own business. He needs some money to begin with, but if his business idea is sound it is usually possible to borrow capital. A shopkeeper, for instance, can buy a shop or rent it and fill it with goods for sale. Suppose it costs him £x to buy the stock, he must charge more than £x when he sells to customers. He needs the extra money to pay wages to his assistants, and to himself, the rent on the building, and to pay back the loan with which he started. A shopkeeper may work very hard and pay himself very little at first. Then when the shop prospers he can afford to pay himself a larger share out of his takings. If customers don't come to the shop, his stock of goods gets old and stale, he cannot pay the rent, or pay back the original loan, and he has no surplus money to live on himself. Then he may go bankrupt. A great many shopkeepers do go bankrupt because they run their businesses badly, or sometimes because they cannot meet competition from other shops. If a big supermarket opens across the road from a small grocer, customers may prefer to go to the big shop. The supermarket can buy stock more cheaply, because it buys in great bulk. The small shop has to cut its prices to bring people in. Cutting prices means smaller profits, and if cuts are severe it might mean no profits at all, or even a loss (see the assignment on p. 35). A man who chooses to run his own business takes a risk. He may get very rich; or he may lose all the money he started with and be worse off than before.

Competition between shops may be good for customers if it keeps prices down. Even when several shops charge the same price for something, a customer can choose between them and may prefer the one which is cleaner, or the one where he gets friendly service. Capitalists say that this freedom is very important and that it is the more efficient shops and businesses that keep going, while the inefficient ones go bankrupt. This, again, does not always work out as it should, and the law frequently has to step in. All the shops in one city might agree to charge unreasonably high prices for some essential commodity, and the customers are then unable to buy it anywhere else. It is quite common for shopkeepers to sell goods underweight to make bigger profits. Such practices are against the law.

In communist states, particularly the U.S.S.R., the shops are generally owned by the government. This means that no one makes a profit, so there is no reason for anyone to over-charge. But there is no competition between shops either, nor between the factories that make the goods for sale. The government has a 'monopoly' of all products and commodities. The government does not build a whole row of shops where one will do; the customer has to buy from the state shops or go without. In Russia, if he does not like the goods, he can't cross the road or go round the corner to another shop. There is only one. The people working in the shop, so long as they do their jobs adequately, don't have to go out of their way to be polite or to help customers. They know the customer will have to keep coming anyway. In China, small shops are encouraged to compete with one another, and shopkeepers take great pride in achieving high sales. Whereas in capitalist shops there may be many different sorts of products to choose from, made by different companies and all at different prices, a government shop tends to sell only one variety—the government variety—of anything, on a take-it-or-leave-it basis. There is much less freedom, but as a rule the costs are lower. Read more about monopolies on p. 33.

Photo. 41 A typical U.S. supermarket. Note the advertising and the variety of goods. Through self-service the supermarket is able to reduce labour costs

Photo. 42 A small department store in China. Shop assistants serve behind the counter

Photo. 43 New York City transport workers out on strike

The working man

Workers in factories or on farms in the U.S.A. know that, as a rule, the profits of their work will go to the factory owner, usually a large company and its shareholders. They will draw their wages at the end of the week, and will almost invariably belong to a trade union which campaigns for increased wages, better working conditions, and shorter working hours. Unions in the U.S.A., as in other capitalist countries, may call their men out on strike, in the hope that such action will achieve these objectives. In the Soviet Union and China, strikes are unknown. The trade unions are, like almost everything else, under the control of the Communist Party, which also runs the government, which is the employer. In theory, workers, unions, and party all co-operate. However, it must often be the case that a worker or group of workers is dissatisfied with pay or conditions. There is very little that can be done about this. In the communist countries there are many workers' meetings, but these are usually restricted to lectures and discussions on the political ideas of the country's leaders.

Monopolies

Where someone, whether it is the state or a huge corporation, has a monopoly of some type of goods, the customer in the shop has very little choice. It is quite common under capitalism for one factory to turn out products with several different labels, so that, for example, the same sugar may go into several different bags with different brand names, or the same sort of tobacco into several different brands of cigarette. The customer can usually find out, if he takes the trouble, when this happens, but often he may believe he is getting a wider choice of goods than he really is. He may sometimes be misled, by advertising, into thinking that Brand X is better than Brand Y, when really the two commodities are exactly the same, made even in the same factory, and only the label is different. To help customers in the U.S.A., various associations exist to examine and test products, and to make known the real differences between them.

In Chinese factories there are numerous banners and large posters calling on the people to work hard for the sake of their country's development. Wages are low, but the worker who produces more than is expected is greatly praised and may be granted special privileges. In the Soviet Union workers may earn special medals and awards, not only for working exceptionally hard, but also for developing some new idea to increase production or improve the quality of a product. It is also possible for a worker who is considered lazy to be criticized at a public meeting.

In the U.S.A. successful businesses sometimes grow very large indeed. They may buy up and take over their competitors, or force most of them out of business. A single company may become so powerful that it comes to control a high proportion of a vital industry, gaining a monopoly of some commodity or product. Such huge corporations and companies, employing many thousands of people and dealing in billions of dollars, have a great deal of influence on the government of the U.S.A. The leaders of big business and of the government keep in close touch because the needs of industry cannot be overlooked by the politicians, whichever political party is in control. The large trade unions, representing the workers in the various industries, also make sure that their interests are recognized by the state. The fate of the country and of its profit-making industries are very much bound up together, so although the degree of control is not so great as it is in the communist countries, government and business are not entirely unconnected. For the ordinary man, working in a state-owned industry, or working for a big corporation, may not feel very different. Under capitalism, however, a man has the *right* to change his job, to start a business of his own, or to work for a small concern where he can have more influence. He also runs the risk of being made redundant and being unemployed. After reading the later chapters in this book you may be able to decide for yourself whether communism and capitalism are as different as they seem at first, or whether in some ways, the two systems are quite alike.

Photo. 44 Lenin Library station on the Moscow underground railway

Assignments

1. Find out in your own home district whether any properties or businesses are state owned, or controlled by the local authority. Would it make very much difference if they were owned privately? Consider the railways, the post office, hospitals, schools, mines, housing estates, and farm land. Sometimes government and private ownership go side by side. Find out what differences there are between:

    council and privately-owned housing;
    private and government hospitals;
    private and state schools;
    independent and state-owned broadcasting (e.g., I.T.V. & B.B.C.);
    public and private libraries;
    state-owned and independent airlines;
    private and municipal buses;
    private farms and national parks and commons.

Consider not only the cost of each to the customer, but also the quality of what can be obtained. What would the effect be if the government took charge of everything, or if it sold all its concerns to private people and companies?

2. Discuss whether private companies could take over and successfully operate the following:

    the army, navy, and airforce;
    roads and highways;
    water supply;
    post office;
    police;
    fire brigade.

(Note that at one time all these were privately owned to some extent. For example, great lords used to have their own armies, private security guards are still common, and at one time fire brigades were owned by insurance companies.)

3. Draw up a table showing how a small shopkeeper uses the money he takes from his customers. With your friends, make a list of all the things he must pay for, for example, buying stock for the shop, paying off instalments on his bank loan, paying rent and rates, paying wages, paying for advertising in the local newspaper, paying electricity bills, taxes, insurance, repairs and upkeep of the shop, telephone, etc. Find out, if possible, the 'wholesale' prices on some common goods in your local shops, and compare them with 'retail' prices charged to customers. After all 'overheads' have been paid for, the profit to the shopkeeper is what he has left. Suggest ways in which a shopkeeper might increase his profits, or ways in which he might fail in his business.

4. Large companies in capitalist countries are managed by boards of directors who may, or may not, own shares in the company. The shareholders buy their shares through a stockbroker in the stock exchange. The profits made by the company are shared out to the shareholders in proportion to the value of the shares held. Find out what you can about this system, and from the business section of a newspaper or magazine, obtain some share prices and some company reports. The value of shares tends to vary from day to day. Make a graph of such changes for a company listed in the newspaper tables. Can you suggest ways in which someone trading in stocks and shares might either lose, or make, money?

Photo. 45 The Customs Hall at Kennedy Airport, New York. The airport is state controlled. What would happen if air terminals in large cities were built by private individuals?

Fig. 4 (a) The republics of the Soviet Union (b) The states of the U.S.A. (c) The administrative units of China

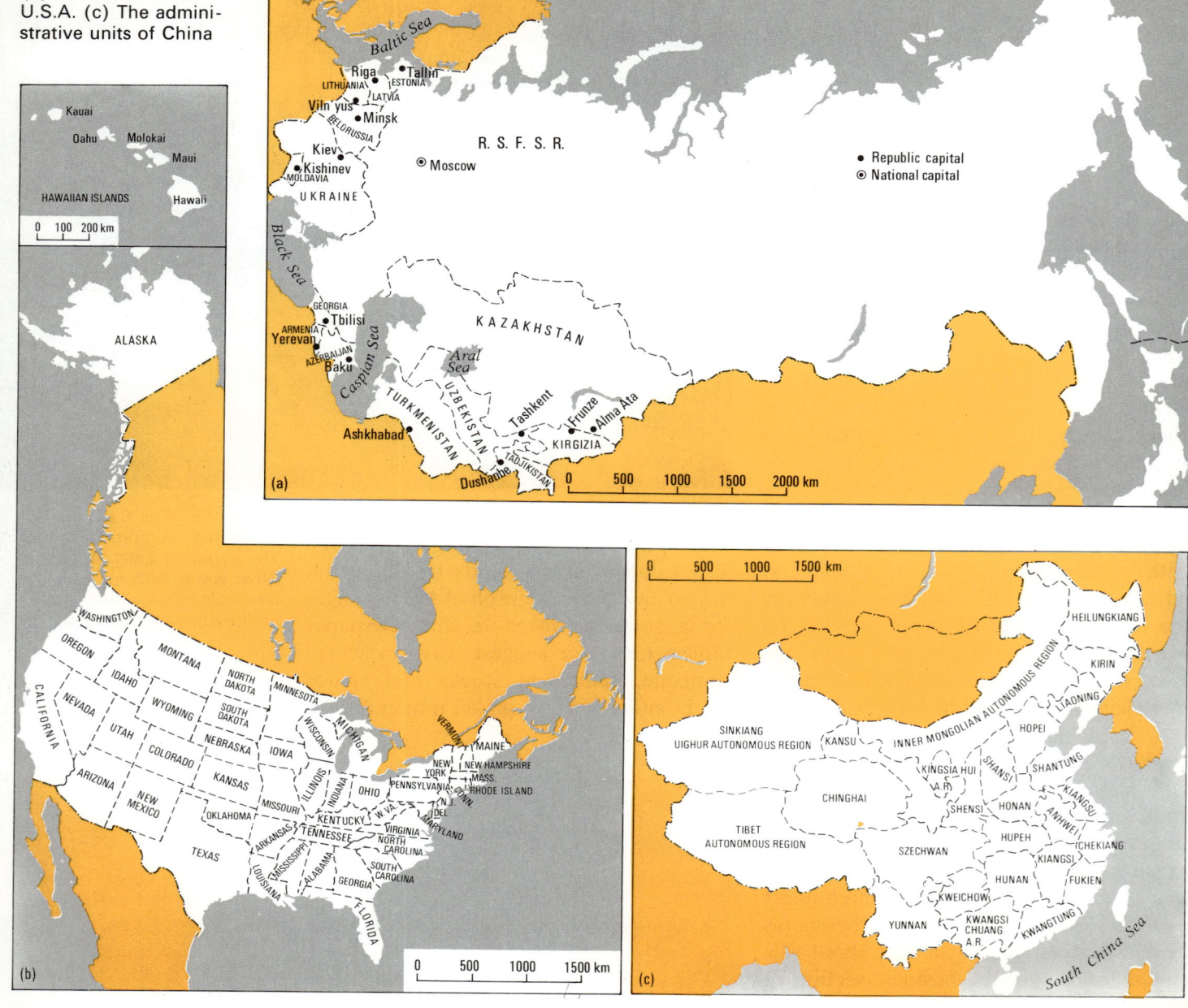

3 Controlling the Giants

To govern a country as large as any one of the three giants is very difficult. People in different regions, particularly those far away from the capital city, tend to think of themselves as different from the rest and, indeed, very often they *are* different, as Chapter 5 shows. Problems which arise in such areas may not be understood by a central government, and cannot be dealt with efficiently from a distance. Yet for the whole country to be held together, it is necessary for each region to belong to it and to come under central control. How have the three great powers tackled this problem?

U.S.A.

The U.S.A., whose form of government is called a republic, is a federation of fifty separate **states**, as its name, the **United States of America**, suggests. The national capital is at Washington D.C., and there is a **President** elected by the whole nation. Each of the fifty states is also like a small nation. Each state has a capital city; Atlanta is the capital of Georgia, Salt Lake City is the capital of Utah. Each state has its own government, and its own elected governor. Many laws are made by the states themselves, and apply only within the state. For example, traffic laws, marriage and divorce laws, laws about the sale and manufacture of alcoholic drink, are likely to be different from state to state. Each state has its own police force and law courts, and to some extent is run like a separate country. In addition, all the states have at some time agreed to join the United States, the latest to do so being Hawaii, and Alaska, both in 1959. It is not impossible that other countries, at present independent, could ask to join the Federation at some future time. Each state elects two senators who go to the upper house or **Senate**, and, as well, the states elect congressmen who go to the **House of Representatives**. The number of congressmen for any state depends on its population.

Although the Washington government makes laws which apply over the whole of the U.S.A., has its own federal police force (the F.B.I.), and controls the armed forces and all relationships between the U.S.A. and the rest of the world, in their day-to-day lives, most Americans are more affected by their local governments than by decisions made in Washington.

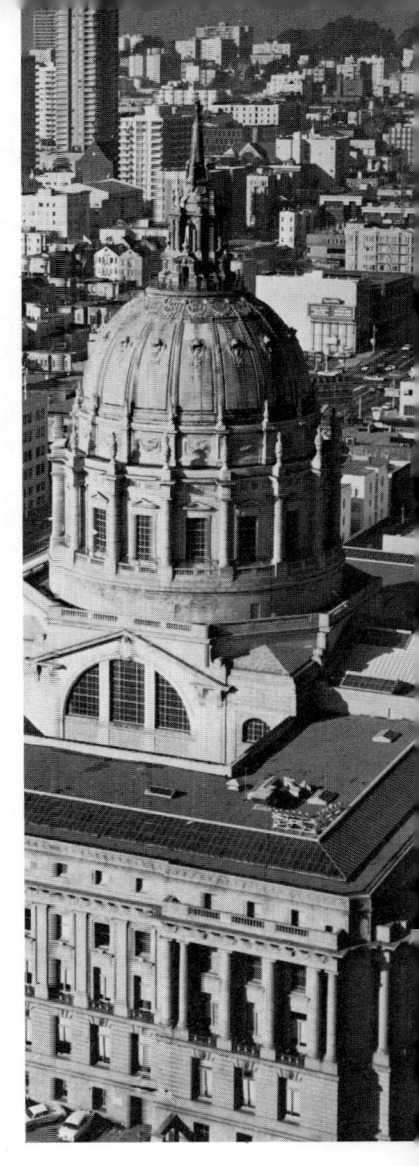

Photo. 46 San Francisco's City Hall. In the larger cities, states may turn certain powers over to the municipal authorities. The City Hall houses offices of city police, city courts, city schools, and other local government services.

Photo. 47 The Supreme Soviet assembles for a few days each year in Moscow. Delegates from every Soviet Republic attend. Approximately a third of the delegates are women

Photo. 48 A meeting of the board of management of a Soviet collective farm. The chairman explains his plans on a map of the farm. A portrait of Lenin hangs on the wall

U.S.S.R.

The U.S.S.R. is also a federation of more or less separate states, each of which is a **republic** with the power to make certain laws and organize local affairs. There are fifteen Soviet Socialist Republics in the **Union of Soviet Socialist Republics** (the largest by far being Russia itself), each with its own capital. Some of these republics—such as Latvia, Lithuania, and Estonia—were once separate countries, and were taken over by force during the period of the Second World War. Another republic, the Ukraine, with its capital, Kiev, has in some ways an even longer history than Russia (see p. 60).

Each village or collective farm or city district has its own council, which is called a **soviet**, and each republic has its own soviet which corresponds in some ways to the governments of the separate states in the U.S.A. The members are elected by the people, but usually the only candidates in the election are persons named by the Communist Party, so there really is no choice. Everyone has to vote, but there is only one party to vote for. In Moscow, for a few days each year, the **Supreme Soviet** meets. This is attended by delegates from every republic of the Union and representatives of every national group. In some ways, therefore, the U.S.S.R. resembles the U.S.A., but the true power in the U.S.S.R. is the Communist Party. The Party elects a central committee of between 100 and 200 members, and from this group are chosen the **Presidium** of about 20. It is the Presidium of the Communist Party which really governs the country, its decisions are passed through to the Central Committee, and then to the local branches of the party, which exist in every farm, factory, school, and office throughout the U.S.S.R.

China

China, like the U.S.S.R., is controlled by its Communist Party, but the country is divided into **provinces**, or regions, which have some degree of control over their own areas. A province in China, like a state of the U.S.A., manages most of its local affairs and the regional government may take many decisions affecting its own people. This is particularly important for areas where the people are of different races, speaking different languages, from the main part of China. Some of these regions are self ruling or **autonomous**, others are expected to become so in time. They are called **Autonomous Chou**, **Autonomous Hsien** and **Autonomous ch'i**. The ancient country of Tibet which the Chinese control, is also intended to be given some autonomy in future years. As in the U.S.S.R. and U.S.A., control of all foreign affairs, and of the military forces, is in the hands of the central government, which in China is in Peking.

Assignments

1. The three giants are not the only countries ruled as federations. Investigate for yourself other large countries such as Canada, Brazil, Australia, India, Mexico, and Argentina, and some smaller ones such as Yugoslavia, Switzerland, and New Zealand.

Are any of the smaller countries run on federal lines? What advantages and disadvantages can you see in such arrangements?

Photo. 49 This shepherd is a member of the Yi nationality, one of China's big minority groups (see Chapter 5). He lives in the self-ruling Liangshan Autonomous Chou of Szechwan Province in southwest China

4 Variety of Land and Climate

The three maps, Fig. 2 (see p. 14), show the population distribution in China, the U.S.A. and the U.S.S.R. The three are alike in one very important respect; in spite of their great numbers of people all have huge areas which are almost empty. In these areas the population density is very low. In other words, comparatively few people are scattered over very great spaces.

The photographs in this chapter give many clues to explain this lack of settlement. Each of the three great powers has regions of desert, high mountains, and areas of bitterly cold climate.

Deserts

The deserts are shown in Fig. 5. The Chinese and Soviet deserts are part of a great belt of arid land that stretches across

Photo. 50 Heavy trucks transport goods across the Gobi Desert

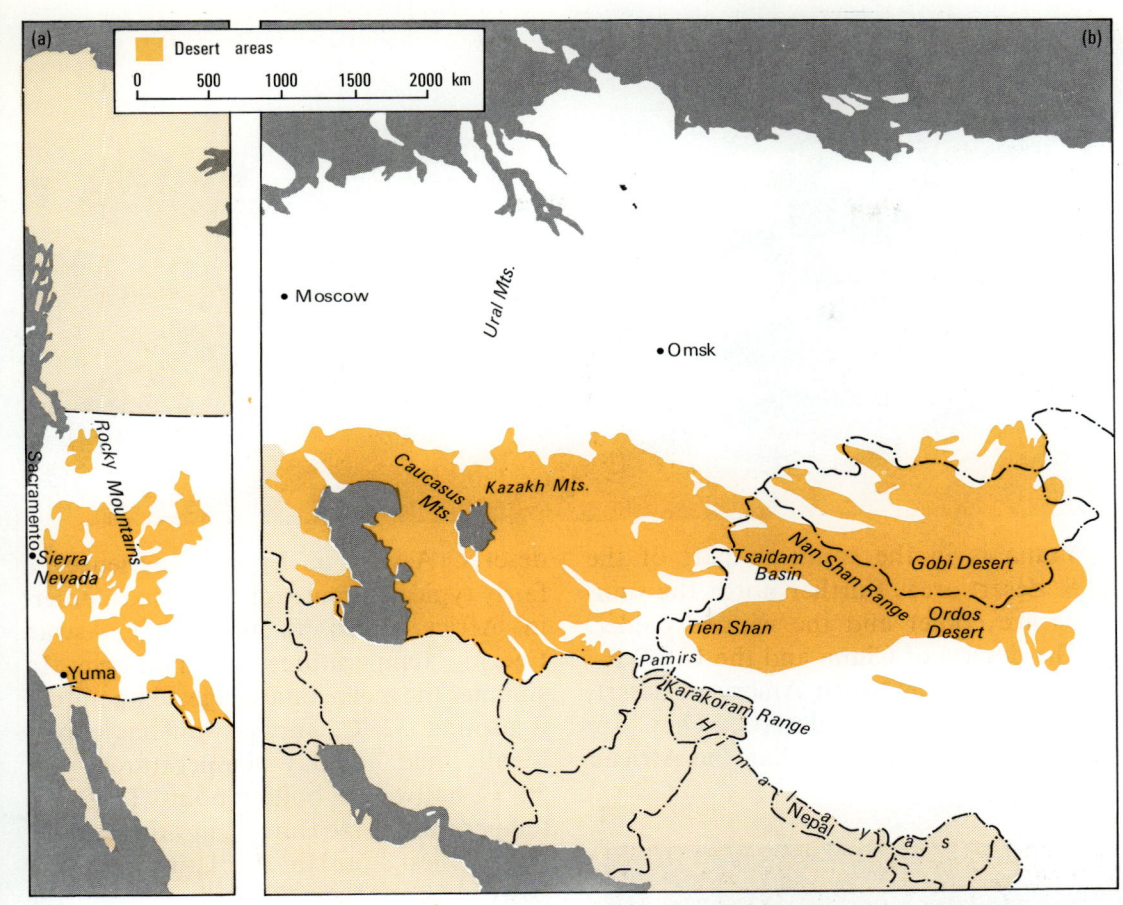

Fig. 5a Desert areas of the U.S.A.

Fig. 5b Desert areas of China and the U.S.S.R.

the whole of central Asia and into Arabia and Africa. The deserts of the U.S.A. are separated from this belt, but conditions are very similar.

In these desert areas there is a great difference between the hottest month of summer and the coldest of winter. The winter months have temperatures well below freezing in most cases, while in summer the temperature is usually well above 20°C. These are mean temperatures. Day-to-day variations will in all cases look similar to those shown on the graph for Yuma, Arizona (Fig. 6). In July it is not uncommon for the temperature at Yuma to rise to 40 °C in the early afternoon. In winter, freezing temperatures may occur at night, and the day may be above 20 °C. If the coldest night of winter is compared with the hottest day of summer, the **range** of temperature may be from below freezing to 45 °C.

Photo. 51 Prospectors set out with mule carts from a railway station in the Gobi Desert. The train goes from Lanchow to Yumen

Fig. 6 Comparison of winter and summer temperatures in the desert region of Yuma, Arizona

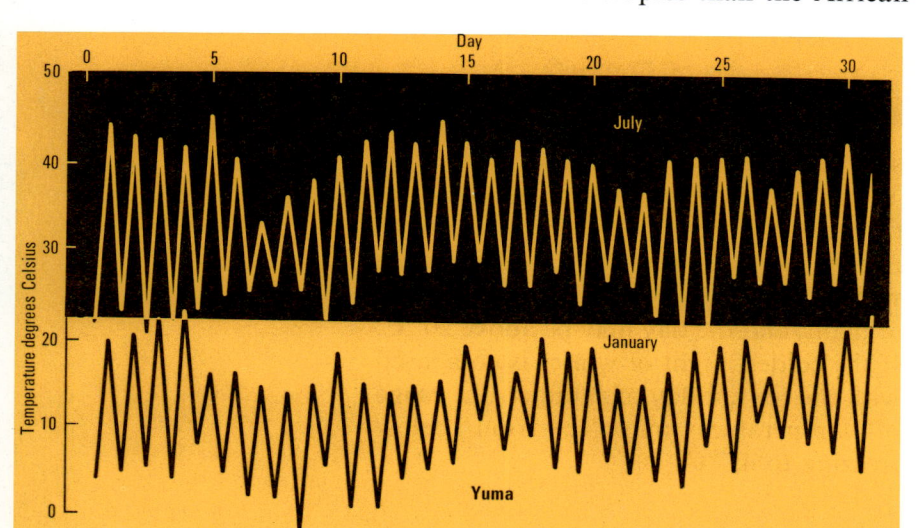

Yuma is in the southern part of the U.S. desert area. Further north the summers are cooler and the winters colder.

The deserts of China and the U.S.S.R., and most of the North American desert, are called the cold deserts. They are further from the tropics than the African deserts. Aswan in Egypt experiences a fairly typical climate for the Sahara desert in Africa. Even in winter at Aswan freezing temperatures are unknown. In summer the mean, or average, temperature is around 32 °C, and Aswan has occasionally had midday temperatures over 50 °C, halfway to boiling point. These are temperatures measured in the shade. Aswan lies close to the latitude of 24° North, i.e., about 2700 km from the Equator. The cold deserts in Asia lie about 45°N, 5000 km from the Equator, and the American deserts are around 40°N, 4500 km north of the Equator. Such cold deserts are in many ways even more difficult to live in than the hot African desert. They are nearly as dry, but in addition are bitterly cold with piercing, dusty winds and when water is found it may well be frozen. It is not surprising that the population maps show these regions to be nearly empty of people.

Photo. 52 The All American Canal in the Imperial Valley in California. This area of desert is known as the 'American Sahara'

Photo. 53 (right, above) Sandy desert land of the south-western U.S.S.R.

Photo. 54 The south-western desert of the U.S.A. in New Mexico. This formation of bare rock surrounded by rock plains is known as Shiprock

In beginning to make use of their cold desert lands, the problems facing the three powers are very similar. They have to bring water into the dry zone in some way, to purify the salty water that is often found underground in dry areas. They have to find ways of improving the dusty and salty soils, and develop new farming methods. In the U.S., modern agriculture, industry, and recreation have made great progress in some areas of the desert. There has been some development in the U.S.S.R., but less progress has been made in China.

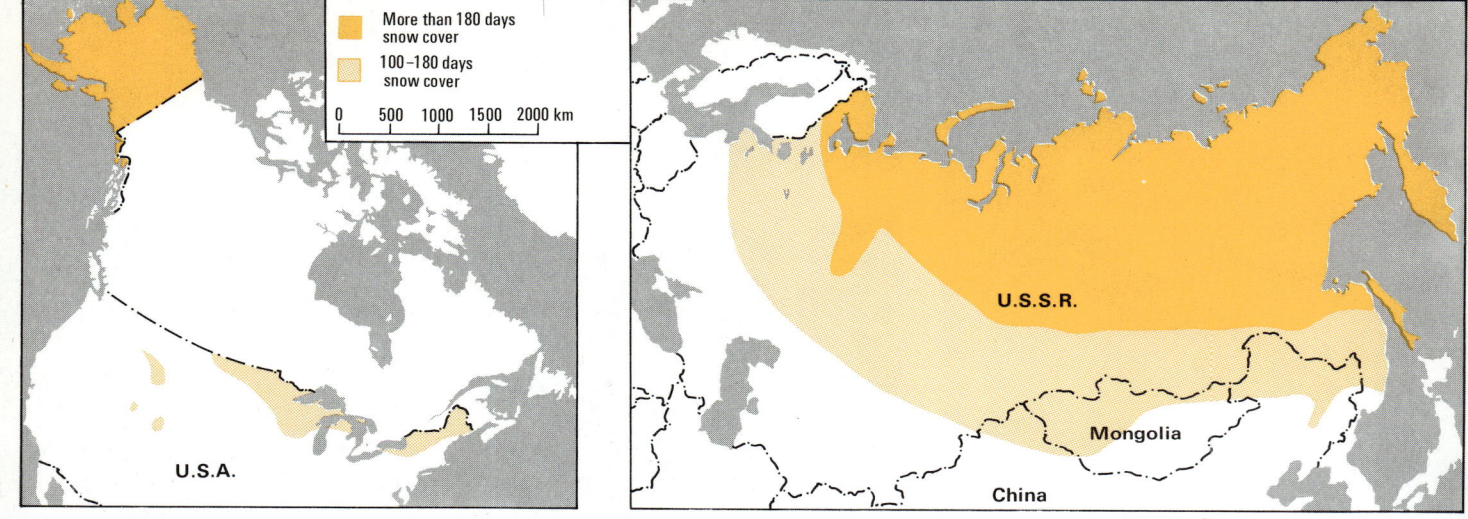

Fig. 7 Snow cover, in days per year, in the U.S.A., China and the U.S.S.R.

Photo. 55 (left) Alaskans of the U.S. travel over the snow using dog teams

Photo. 56 (right) Dog teams in the U.S.S.R. deliver mail that is carried in by helicopter

Bitter cold

In south China and south U.S.A. winter brings only one or two days of snow, and sometimes none at all. Further north the snow usually lies on the ground, covering it for several weeks. In the far north-east of China it is usual for snow cover to last for more than 100 days, over a quarter of the year. In the north-east of the U.S.A. the same is true. Compare these areas with the U.S.S.R., and with the U.S. state of Alaska. Over huge areas, snow cover lasts longer than three months every year, and further north again winter lasts more than half the year. Note carefully the areas which lie beyond the 180 days' snow cover zone.

Consider what the long and bitter

winters mean to people living in such climates. Water in lakes and rivers freezes completely and remains frozen for months. No plants will grow out of doors, and work on farms comes to a complete standstill. When the thaw comes, at first everything is wet and there may be floods as the snow and ice melt. Then there will be only a few weeks of the summer left before snow falls again. In the coldest areas, there is not sufficient time for the thaw to penetrate far into the ground, so the soil is frozen for many metres down. This is called **permafrost**. Trees with deep roots cannot survive. If houses are built on such land and heated, the warmth begins to thaw the soil beneath the walls and the house begins to crack and settle into the ground unless special foundations are designed.

Few people would choose to live in such a harsh environment as this, and although there are—in Alaska and the northern parts of the U.S.S.R.—some mines and oil wells, it is hardly surprising that such regions remain largely unsettled.

Photo. E7 The plains of northern Siberia, a land of bitter cold in the winter, and swamps in the summer

Photo. E8 A Soviet prospecting team in the mountains of southern Siberia

Photo. 59 (left) A mountaineering expedition in the Himalaya region of south-west China

Photo. 60 The Rocky Mountains in Colorado

Mountains

High mountainous regions are always very difficult for man. Not only is it hard to get from place to place, but the climate is always colder than on the lowlands, there is little flat land for building or farming, and soils tend to be thin and stony. In the highest and coldest places there are often permanent snowfields and glaciers. Most of the western states of the U.S.A. are mountainous. The Rocky Mountains in Colorado and Wyoming, and the Sierra Nevada ranges in California, exceed 3500 metres; in Alaska, Mt. McKinley is over 6000 metres high. Notice that much of this mountain country is also desert land. The same pattern is found in China, though the mountains of the west are even higher and the desert conditions are even more severe. It is in fact partly the mountains which create the deserts, since the high ranges block the moisture-carrying air from the oceans.

Western China contains vast mountain ranges including parts of the Himalayas, the highest in the world. Mt. Everest itself, over 8800 metres high, is on China's border with Nepal, and there are hundreds of other mighty peaks almost as high, in the Karakoram and Nan Shan ranges. Between these ice-covered ridges are high valleys, often full of ice, and plateaux at above 3500 metres.

The Soviet Union has fewer high mountains, though the frontier with China follows some of the great ranges in the Pamirs and Tien Shan. The Caucasus Mountains, between the Black Sea and the Caspian, are over 3500 metres, but their area is small compared with the Chinese and American mountain regions. The Ural Mountains of the U.S.S.R. are comparatively low, reaching 1900 metres in a few places, but mostly being below 1000 metres.

Assignments

1. Make a tracing in pencil or black ink of the mountainous areas in each of the three countries. Using the same tracing paper, mark the areas of desert climates in yellow crayon. With a blue crayon shade the regions with cold winter (more than 100 days snow cover). Lay this tracing over the population map. What reasons can you now give for the vast areas of small population? Are there any surprises, places you would expect to find deserted which do in fact have large settlements? If so, make a note of them. You may be able to discover reasons for these exceptions from an encyclopaedia or other reference book. To assist you, consider some of the reasons given below why people might sometimes choose to live in areas with uncomfortable climate or difficult location:

- they may be mining for rare minerals or oil;
- they may have been driven into such areas in the first place by enemies;
- the area may be important to their religion;
- the area may be very beautiful and attractive to tourists and holiday makers (e.g., winter sports centres);
- military bases are often placed far from the centre of a country, either to defend its frontiers or to give ample room for exercises and practice bombing.

Three important places you should consider are: Lhasa in China, Salt Lake City in the U.S.A., and Vorkuta in the U.S.S.R.

Photo. 61 In the high mountains of north-east China, girl soldiers maintain and service communications by repairing telephone wires

Photo. 62 (right above) Polar night over Vorkuta coalfield in the U.S.S.R. For several months of the winter the sun never rises

Photo. 63 Salt Lake City, capital of Utah

47

Fig. 8 Temperature and rainfall in Sacramento, California, U.S.A.

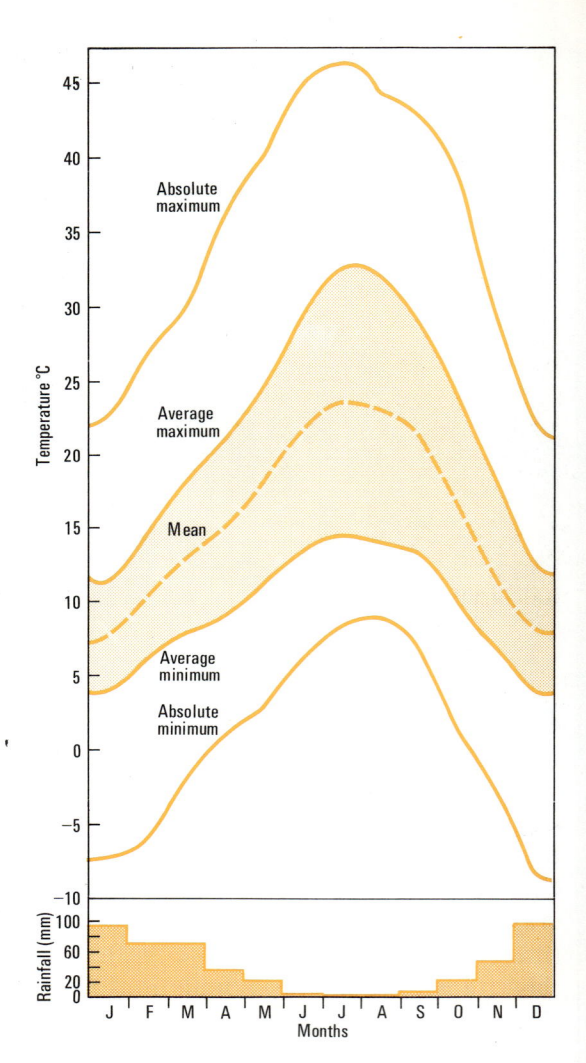

Climates in the populated regions

In studying the climate of populated areas much detail is needed. Fig. 8 illustrates the climate of Sacramento in California (U.S.A.). Sacramento has been chosen because it has a climate very different from any places in China or the U.S.S.R. Of the three great powers, only the U.S.A. has a long coastline facing westwards. The western frontiers of both China and the U.S.S.R. are *land* frontiers. This makes a big difference to the climate.

South-west coast U.S.A.

Records of temperature and rainfall have been kept at Sacramento for many years. The coldest temperature ever measured at night is just below −8 °C, eight degrees below freezing. The hottest ever recorded is 45°. The total range of temperature is thus about 53 degrees, from the coldest winter night to the hottest summer day ever known during the time records have been kept. The record figure for each month of the year is given in the graph by the upper and lower line, labelled 'Absolute maximum' and 'Absolute minimum'. In July, for instance, the temperature at night has never been known to fall below 8°. Such record temperatures are rare; when they occur people get excited and the figures are mentioned by the newspapers, radio and T.V. As a rule in Sacramento an ordinary summer day is cooler than 45°, something like 32° would be more likely, and at night the thermometer would fall to about 14 or 15°. Average day and night temperatures for each period of the year are shown on the graph by the lines marked 'Average maximum' and 'Average minimum'. The area between these two lines has been shaded to indicate that most of the time in Sacramento the temperature will be somewhere between the average readings. Anything far outside this shaded zone will be rather unusual.

Midway between the average maximum and the average minimum is the 'mean' temperature for the month, and the line joining these mid-points is the one usually drawn to illustrate the climate of an area. Such graphs of mean temperature tend to hide the day-to-day variations which affect people most. For example, a fruit grower needs to know how often he can expect frost at night. In Sacramento frosts have never been recorded in April or in October, which gives seven months free from frost.

At the foot of the graph is shown the average rainfall for Sacramento. Notice that although there is quite a lot of rain in the winter and early spring, the summer is very dry. In July, the hottest month, there is usually less than 2·0 mm of rainfall. Like the mean temperature graph, the average rainfall figures conceal day-to-day or year-to-year variations. A single freak storm might bring 20 or 30 mm in a few hours.

Sacramento's climate, with hot, dry summers, is typical of the south-west coast of the U.S.A. China has nothing like this anywhere, and the U.S.S.R. in the far south near the Black Sea coast, has only a very small region which is similar, and even this is much wetter than Sacramento in summer and cooler in winter.

Photo. 64 The Californian climate, which is known as a 'Mediterranean climate', is suitable for growing grapes, but an unexpected frost can destroy a whole crop. This device, a heater with propellers, scatters cold air before it can damage the vines

Photo. 65 Holiday makers in Miami play cards in the hot sun

Fig. 9 Comparison of climate recorded in Miami, U.S.A., and Omsk, U.S.S.R.

Contrasts of climate

Graphs of this kind can be used to compare two places. Omsk in the U.S.S.R. and Miami in the U.S.A. are shown on Fig. 9. The record temperatures (Absolute maximum and Absolute minimum) have been left out, and so has the 'mean'. Only the average conditions are shown, the coloured shading indicates the average temperatures for Omsk, the grey shading for Miami. Obviously these two cities experience very different climates.

In Miami on an average winter day the temperature reaches about 23 or 24° and at night falls to about 16 °C. In Omsk, even at the warmest time of day in winter, the temperature is likely to remain around −18°, eighteen degrees below freezing, and at night it drops still further. The winters in Miami, even at night, are similar to the summer days at Omsk. Omsk is obviously a very much colder place at any time of the year than Miami, but note also that in Omsk the *range* of temperature, from highest to lowest, is very great whereas in Miami it is rather small.

The graph of rainfall also shows great contrasts. Omsk is much drier than Miami at all times. However, there is one point of similarity—the summer months in both places are wetter than the winter. But the fall in winter in Omsk is in the form of snow, quite unlike the warm rainfall of Miami. Note that Omsk is very far from the sea. (Find it on an atlas map.)

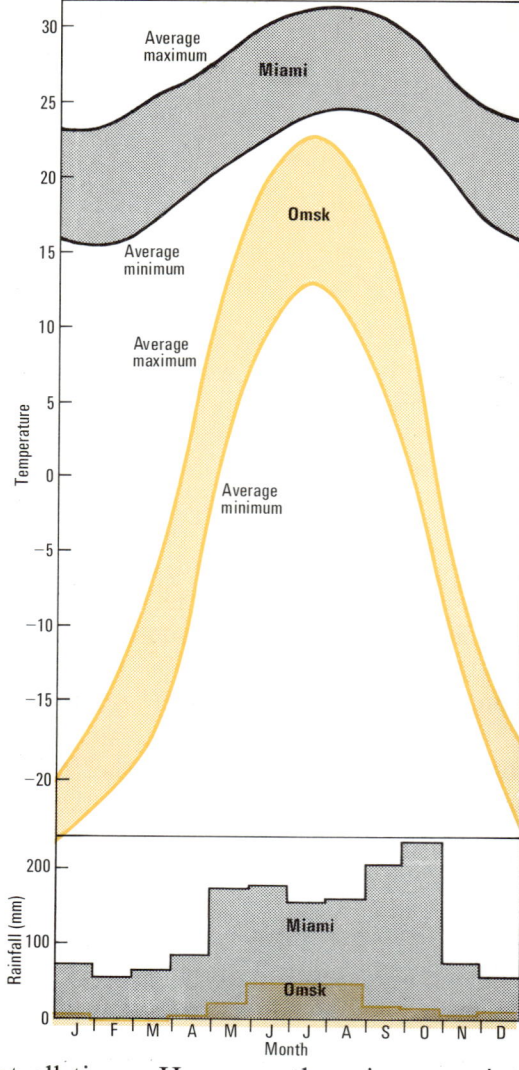

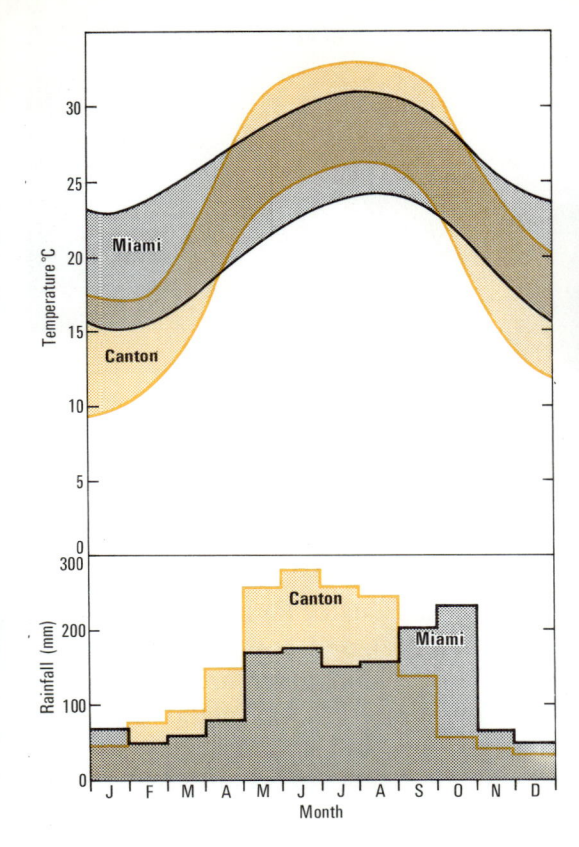

The next graph is a comparison of Miami with Canton, in southern China. The two shaded areas this time overlap a great deal. In winter Canton tends to be somewhat cooler than Miami and in summer it is a few degrees warmer, but on the whole the two places are very similar. The rainfall graph also shows similarities. Canton and Miami both have most of their rainfall in the summer. Canton is wetter in the months from April to August, and Miami's highest rainfall comes later in the summer, but broadly the pattern is similar.

It is fair to say that Miami and Canton have similar climates. Find them in an atlas. Canton is close to the south-eastern coast of China. The Pacific Ocean lies to the east and the South China Sea to the south. The mainland area of China lies to the north-west. Canton is very close to the Tropic of Cancer, which means that in midsummer the noon sun is almost directly overhead. The situation of Miami is remarkably similar. It lies on the coast with the Atlantic Ocean to the east and the Caribbean Sea with its many islands to the south. The mainland lies to the north-west. Miami is some distance north of the Tropic of Cancer which partly accounts for the lower summer temperatures.

The information gained from studying the graph, that these two cities have similar climate, is supported by the map. They are in similar positions in relation to land and ocean, and in relation to the tropics. They are alike in another way

Photo. 66 Summer in Canton. Note that the people walk or use bicycles. Few individuals in China own cars (see Photo. 156)

Fig. 10 (left) Comparison of climate in Canton, China, and in Miami, U.S.A.

Photo. 67 Hurricane damage on the Florida coast

also; both are sometimes struck by very violent wind storms, known as hurricanes in Miami and as typhoons in Canton. These storms bring widespread damage all over the South China Sea region and the Caribbean.

Omsk, in contrast, is very far from any sea, much further north (55°N Lat.) in the heart of the U.S.S.R. Both its climate and position are very different from either Miami or Canton.

No part of China is as far north as Omsk, so it would not be expected that any part of that country would be as cold as Omsk, except perhaps for some areas in the highest mountains. The main northern frontier of the U.S.A. is along the line of 49°N latitude, so most of that country also is well south of the latitude of Omsk. There is a small part of Alaska at 55°N latitude, but this is very close to the sea and is therefore much warmer and wetter than Omsk. Some places in Canada such as Fort Smith and Fort Nelson have similar climate to Omsk, and they, too, are far inland and north of Latitude 55°N. Find them in an atlas.

The next graph compares three cities—Washington, U.S.A., Peking, China, and Moscow, U.S.S.R. These are the capital cities of the three great powers. Before studying the graph closely, compare the positions of these cities on the map. Washington and Peking are both about 40°N of the Equator (Washington 38°50′; Peking 39°55′), and both are on the eastern side of the mainland area, not on the coast but about 150 km inland. The temperature graph, as expected, is very similar although Peking appears a little colder in winter. A bigger difference is shown in the rainfall figures. Washington gets a fairly even amount of rain through the year, Peking has a rather dry winter but a period of heavy rain, known as the monsoon, in July and August. The monsoon appears in Canton too and affects the whole of eastern China.

Moscow lies far inland and far to the north. Its climate is colder than that of Peking or Washington. The rainfall comes all year round but rather more in summer than in winter. The winter fall is usually snow. Note from the earlier map (Fig. 7) that Moscow lies in the region with more than 100 days' snow cover.

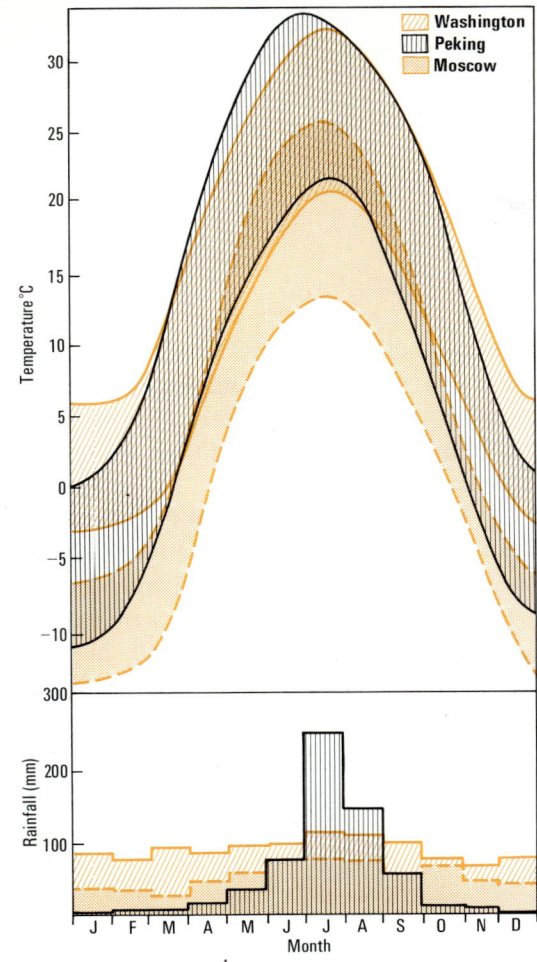

From comparisons of the kind made in this chapter it can be shown that the three great powers do have some areas of very similar climate. Fig. 12 shows these. In what ways are China and the U.S.A. alike? Compare the western regions of each, noting the arrangement of highlands and deserts. Then compare the eastern regions. How can you describe the warm, coastal regions to the south? How do they differ from the coastal regions further north? Does Russia have any areas that could be described as 'near-tropical'?

Assignments

1. Find out, from a reference book, about hurricanes, typhoons and the monsoon. What effect do they have on houses, crops, and shipping?

2. Find out the climatic figures for your own area and graph them in similar fashion to those in this chapter. Compare your graph with those shown here. What reasons can you suggest for the differences? Is there any part of China, the U.S.A., or U.S.S.R. which you would expect to have a similar climate?

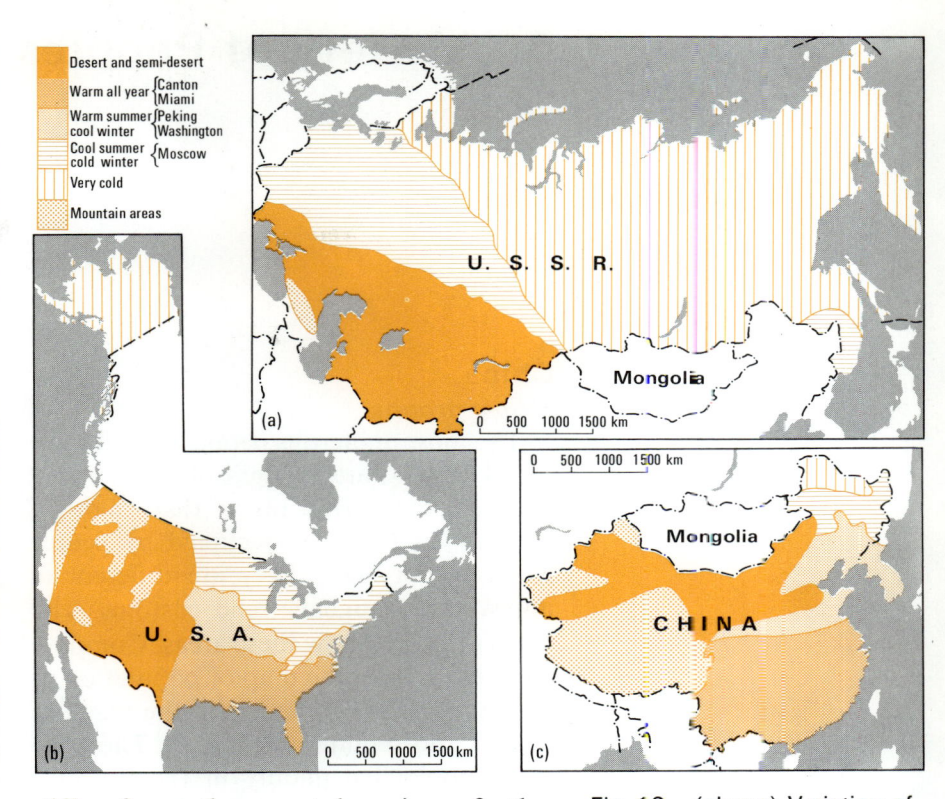

Fig. 12 (above) Variation of climate in (a) the U.S.S.R.; (b) the U.S.A.; (c) China

Fig. 11 (left) Comparison of climate in Washington, Peking and Moscow

5 Variety of Peoples

China
Ethnic groups

The most numerous people in China are the Han, who are thought of as the 'true' Chinese race. But more than half of China's land area is occupied by people who are not Han. They are different in appearance, language, and customs. The maps (Fig. 13) show these areas. Compare these maps with the map of population in Chapter 1 (Fig. 2), and with the maps of deserts and mountains (Fig. 5). The non-Han people live mainly in the western, thinly-peopled regions, and in the south-west near China's frontiers with Thailand, Vietnam and Laos. The Han probably number over 700 million; all the other peoples together are fewer than 50 million.

Language

In the west, languages like Turkish are spoken, and in the north there is a Mongolian tongue. Some of the primitive tribes of the south-west have no written language of their own, so they can have no books, newspapers, or magazines unless they learn another language. The government in Peking sends scholars to live with these people and to design written

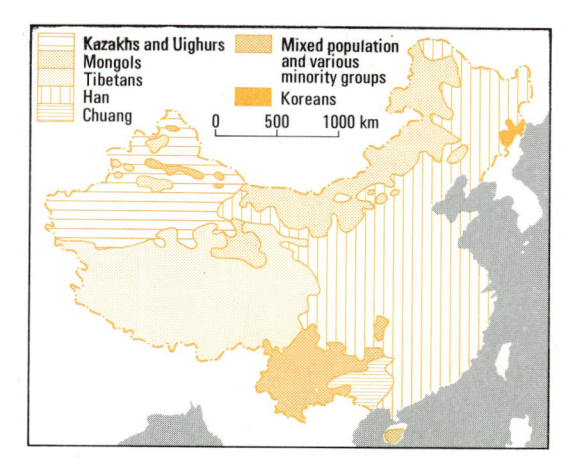

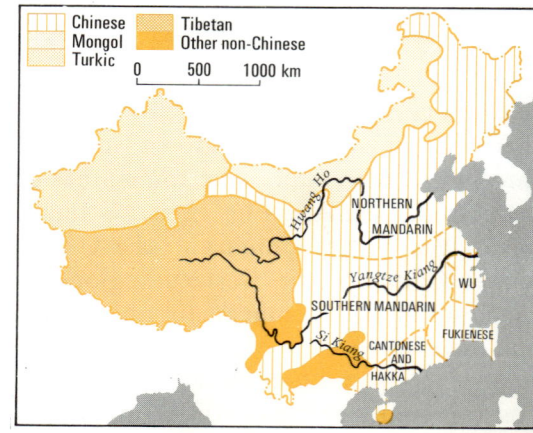

Fig. 13a Major ethnic groups of China

Fig. 13b Broad divisions of language within China

alphabets for them.

Even among the Han themselves there are great differences in language, religion, and customs. The official language of China is Mandarin, which was spoken originally mainly in the north of China around Peking. In many regions Mandarin is not generally understood. Since it has been adopted by the government, children everywhere have to learn it at school, although it is almost a foreign language to some of them. Even Mao Tse-tung, who came from Hunan province in the south, spoke the Hunanese dialect as a child, and because of his strong accent was very rarely heard speaking on the radio. His important speeches were always read for him by someone who spoke the standard form of Mandarin.

The written Chinese language is quite

Photo. 68   A girl of the Tali Pai Autoromous Chou in Yunnan leaps in a traditional dance. The dancers are dressed in the Pai national costume

Photo. 69   A boy of the small Penglung nation of south-west China. He is playing a pipe organ and wearing traditional costume

Photo. 70   A Han woman takes care of her grandson while his parents are working

55

Fig. 14 Chinese words and numbers

Character		Pronunciation	Meaning
ᄼ ᄼ ᄼ ᄼ → 人		jen	man
ᄼ ᄼ ᄼ ᄼ → 手		shou	hand
ᄼ ᄼ ᄼ ᄼ → 日		jih	sun
ᄼ ᄼ ᄼ ᄼ → 魚		yü	fish
ᄼ ᄼ ᄼ → 水		shui	water
ᄼ ᄼ ᄼ → 山		shan	mountain

Character	Pronunciation	Meaning
一	ee	one
二	erh	two
三	sun	three
四	sser	four
五	woo	five
六	leoo	six
七	chee	seven
八	ba	eight
九	jiou	nine
十	sher	ten

different from those of the west. Instead of an alphabet of separate letters which are built up into words, each word or idea is shown by a separate character or **ideograph** (idea-drawing). Sometimes the ideograph is a simplified picture of the thing it represents. The table (Fig. 14) shows how in early Chinese writing, thousands of years ago, the writer actually drew a picture of the thing he wished to record. As years went by such drawings became simpler and simpler, until in modern Chinese the ideograph looks very different from its original form. More complicated words or ideas are represented by more complex characters.

To read Chinese it is necessary to learn by heart a different ideograph for every word. There are more than 40 000 of them, and no single person can know each one. To read an ordinary newspaper the reader must remember about 3000 ideographs and many people never get much beyond this stage in scholarship. One advantage of this style of writing is that the ideographs have the same meaning all over China. People in Canton and Peking, although they *speak* differently and have trouble carrying on a conversation, can write letters to each other easily, using ideographs that both understand, even though they pronounce the words differently.

Religion

The central government in China is, like all strict communist governments, officially opposed to religion. Mao once said: 'Religion is poison'. Any kind of worship is regarded as superstition. In spite of this, many ordinary Chinese folk cling to their beliefs. There are, particularly in the far west of the country, many Moslems, some of whom make the traditional pilgrimage to Mecca at least once in their lives. In Tibet most people are

Buddhists, and there are a vast number of Buddhist shrines and temples throughout the rest of China. Buddhism has no god in the sense of the Christian or Moslem God. Buddha, who was a prince in India hundreds of years before Christ, taught the way of peaceful contemplation and good conduct. There is no single great book of Buddhist scripture; instead there are many books written at different times and places.

Almost all Chinese, even today under the Communist rule, are familiar with the main teachings of Confucius, a wise man born in Shantung 551 years before Christ, who travelled all over China learning and teaching. Confucianism is not a religion. Confucius claimed that the wise man was the best, and learning how to be wise and how to behave well was the proper aim of life for everyone. He said: 'We don't know enough yet about serving men, how can we know anything about service to the gods?'

Photo. 71 The distinctive roof of a Buddhist temple is seen in silhouette against the setting sun

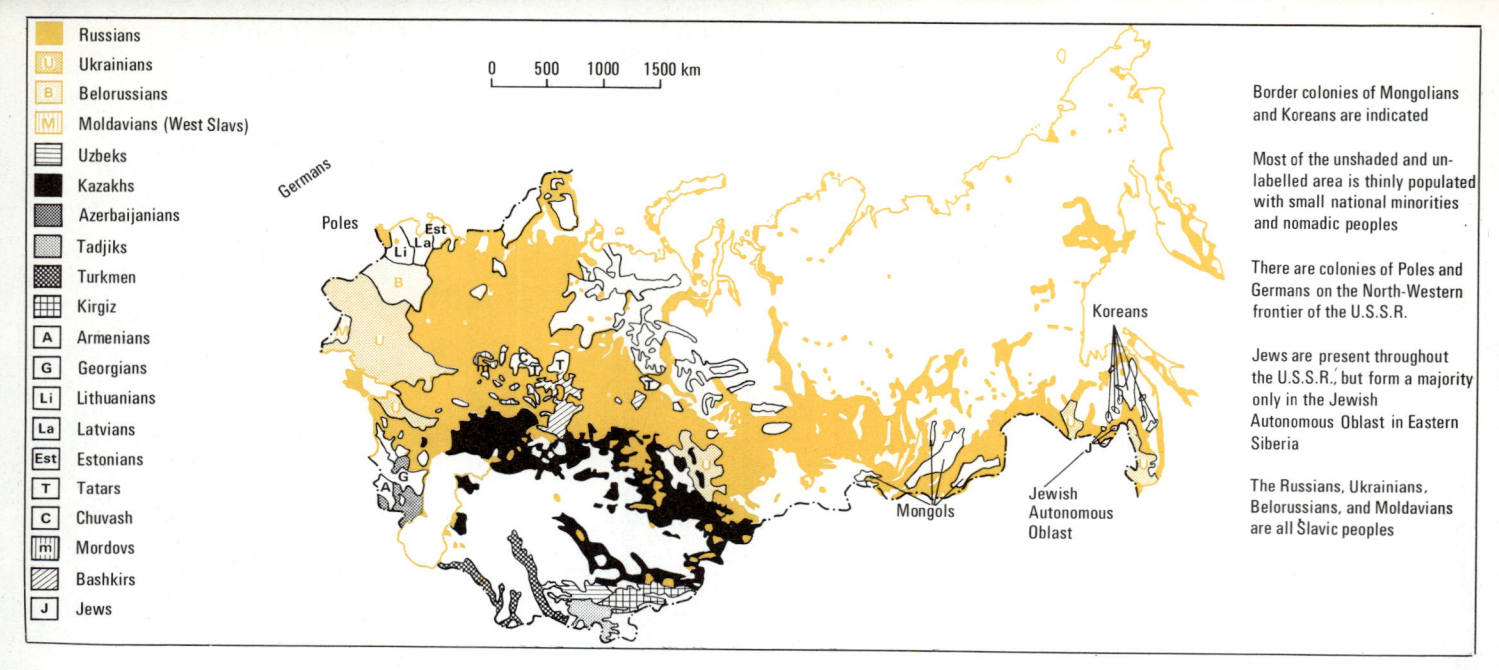

Legend:
- Russians
- U: Ukrainians
- B: Belorussians
- M: Moldavians (West Slavs)
- Uzbeks
- Kazakhs
- Azerbaijanians
- Tadjiks
- Turkmen
- Kirgiz
- A: Armenians
- G: Georgians
- Li: Lithuanians
- La: Latvians
- Est: Estonians
- T: Tatars
- C: Chuvash
- m: Mordovs
- Bashkirs
- J: Jews

Border colonies of Mongolians and Koreans are indicated

Most of the unshaded and unlabelled area is thinly populated with small national minorities and nomadic peoples

There are colonies of Poles and Germans on the North-Western frontier of the U.S.S.R.

Jews are present throughout the U.S.S.R., but form a majority only in the Jewish Autonomous Oblast in Eastern Siberia

The Russians, Ukrainians, Belorussians, and Moldavians are all Slavic peoples

Fig. 15   National groups of the U.S.S.R.

Table 4

	Population in millions	Approximate percentage of total U.S.S.R. population		Population in millions	Approximate percentage of total U.S.S.R. population
Russians	114.1	54.7	Germans	1.6	0.8
Ukrainians	37.3	17.8	Chuvash	1.5	0.7
Belorussians	7.9	3.8	Latvians	1.4	0.7
Uzbeks	6.0	2.9	Poles	1.4	0.7
Tartars	5.0	2.4	Tadjiks	1.4	0.7
Kazakhs	3.6	1.7	Mordovs	1.3	0.6
Azerbaijanians	2.9	1.4	Turkmens	1.0	0.5
Armenians	2.8	1.3	Estonians	1.0	0.5
Georgians	2.7	1.3	Kirgiz	1.0	0.5
Lithuanians	2.3	1.1	Bashkirs	1.0	0.5
Jews	2.3	1.1	Other nationalities	1.6	0.8
Moldavians	2.2	1.0			

U.S.S.R.
Ethnic groups

Like China, the U.S.S.R. contains a great many different ethnic groups; one group, the Russians, is larger than all the rest together, just as the Han are the largest group in China. Whereas the Han make up 90 per cent of the Chinese, the Russians are only a little more than half of all the Soviet citizens. All the other groups of people, whether they differ from the majority in culture, religion, or race, are called **minorities**. A list of the chief nationalities is given in the table on this page, and a map shows their locations (Fig. 15). Note that in some cases, such as the Kazakhs and Koreans, the frontier of China and the U.S.S.R. divides a group into two. There are Kazakhs in western China and Mongols in Manchuria, and these people, speaking the same language and having similar customs, probably feel more at home with the Kazakhs and Mongols of the Soviet Union, than they do with any Han from Peking or any Russian from Moscow.

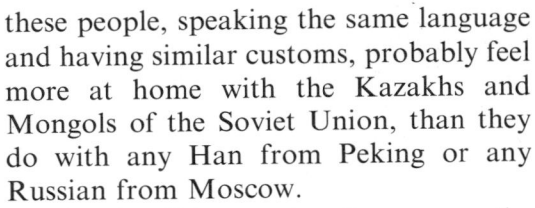

Like the Chinese minority groups, the Soviet minorities tend to occupy areas close to the frontiers; often these regions are the least fertile. The Kazakhs are a desert people, and the Yakuts and Samoyeds dwell chiefly in the cold northern and eastern lands. The Ukrainians are an important exception. The Ukraine is a huge, well-populated area, and includes some of the world's most fertile farming land, known as the 'black earth' belt. Kiev and Kharkov are large and important industrial cities and both have over a million inhabitants.

Photo. 72 Kazakh people are found on either side of the Chinese—U.S.S.R. border. This market scene is at Alma-Ata in the U.S.S.R.

Photo. 73 Mongolian people are found in both China and the U.S.S.R., as well as in the Mongolian People's Republic which lies between the two powers

Photo. 74 A family in Krasnoyarsk in Siberia

Photo. 75 Learning to speak Russian. A kindergarten in Tashkent

Fig. 16 The Russian alphabet

Russian letter		English spelling
А	а	A
Б	б	B
В	в	V
Г	г	G
Д	д	D
Е	е	E
Ё	ё	Ë
Ж	ж	ZH
З	з	Z
И	и	I
Й	й	Ĭ
К	к	K
Л	л	L
М	м	M
Н	н	N
О	о	O
П	п	P
Р	р	R
С	с	S
Т	т	T
У	у	U
Ф	ф	F
Х	х	KH
Ц	ц	TS
Ч	ч	CH
Ш	ш	SH
Щ	щ	SHCH
Ъ	ъ	"
Ы	ы	Ȳ
Ь	ь	'
Э	э	É
Ю	ю	YU
Я	я	YA

Language

The Ukrainian language is close to Russian, but quite difficult for a Russian to follow, in rather the same way as, say, a Scottish accent may be misunderstood in London, or a Londoner in Glasgow. At one time large parts of the Ukraine were completely separate from Russia, ruled from Kiev by great princes. At times also large numbers of German people settled in the Ukraine, bringing with them West European ideas and habits. Even now some Ukrainians feel that they should form an independent country of their own, separate from the Soviet Union. Some felt so strongly about this that they were forced to leave the country, and the same is true of some Armenians and Georgians. Many of these people migrated to the United States (see Photo. 81).

All children in the U.S.S.R. learn Russian at school from the age of seven onwards, if it is not their native tongue. The Russian alphabet developed from Greek rather than Latin, so the letters are not the same as those used in English and other West European languages.

Religion

As in China, the communist government of the U.S.S.R. is opposed to all religion. Young people who wish to make a career for themselves in politics or business are not likely to be promoted rapidly if they openly attend church. Government newspapers frequently print cartoons and articles mocking religion. In spite of this, as in China, some people continue their old beliefs. Among the Kazakhs there are many Moslems, but most religious people in the U.S.S.R. belong to .the Orthodox Church and practise an ancient form of Christianity.

Photo. 76 A priest of the Orthodox Church in Russia

Photo. 77 Moslems pray at a mosque in Samarkand, U.S.S.R.

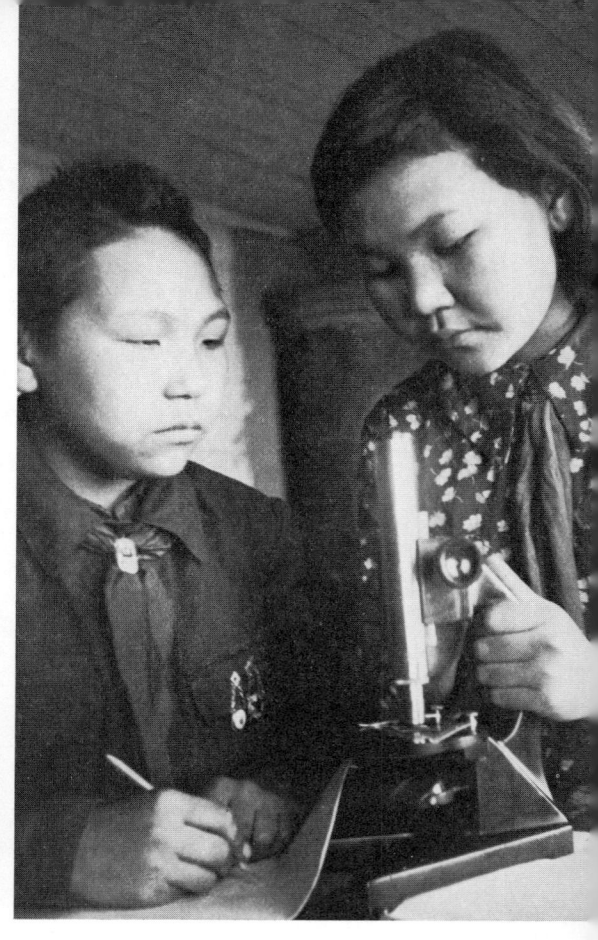

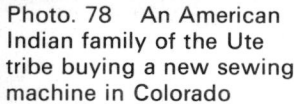

Photo. 78   An American Indian family of the Ute tribe buying a new sewing machine in Colorado

Photo. 79   Eskimo students

U.S.A.
Ethnic groups

The U.S.A. also has great variety of people. Only the Red Indians and the Alaskan Eskimos are native to the land, and the rest of the population have moved into the continent from overseas, most of them from Europe, during the last 350 years.

There are still some American Indians living on reserves in the west, but for the most part they were forced to give way before the advancing Europeans. During their conquest of North America the Europeans brought disease and death to generations of Indians. These 'Indians', having acquired guns from the Europeans, warred against each other, and laid waste to their hunting grounds. Many of their remaining number were killed by Europeans in the great rush for land to the west.

People emigrated from every part of Europe. French settlers came in from Canada and followed the Mississippi River down to the Gulf of Mexico. Note the French names they gave to cities such

Photo. 80 Louisiana was founded by the French in 1699 during the reign of Louis XIV, then came under Spanish rule in the eighteenth century, before returning to France in 1801, and then to the U.S.A. in 1803

as St. Louis, Detroit, New Orleans, and the state Louisiana, named after King Louis of France. Spanish people entered what is now the U.S.A. from Mexico, and the West Indies, christening cities: Los Angeles, San Francisco, and states like Arizona, Florida, and California; and rivers: the Rio Grande and Sacramento. British, Dutch, and German people settled along the Atlantic coast. New York was originally called New Amsterdam, Boston was named after an English town, and Charleston after King Charles.

During the nineteenth and twentieth centuries, millions of people migrated to America from Europe; from England, Ireland and Scotland, from Germany, Scandinavia, Poland, Italy, and Greece, and in the west settlers came in far smaller numbers from Japan and China. Today some of these different groups remain, speaking their own languages and living in their own way, but most now think of themselves simply as Americans, and often the only sign that their ancestors came from Europe is in their surname.

Photo. 81 Many Eastern Europeans migrated to America rather than accept Russian domination of their lands. This family pose proudly in national costume

Photo. 82 Chinatown in New York

Photo. 83 Black children play in the streets of Harlem. Almost no white people live in this part of New York

Fig. 17 (below) Distribution of the black population of the U.S.A.

The most important and obvious minority within the U.S.A. is the Afro-American community. There are over 20 million, about one tenth of the total population. The blacks were brought to the American continent from Africa as slaves, to work as labourers and servants, particularly on the plantations of the south-east. Slavery was abolished in the U.S.A. after the Civil War of 1861 to 1865, but for many years afterwards most former slaves were hardly any better off than before. Today every part of the U.S.A. has some black population. In the cities of the north-east, middle west, and California there are crowded districts, called **ghettos**, where hardly any white people live, and there are some small towns, quite separate from 'white' areas, which are completely black. Half of the black population is still found in the south-eastern parts of the country, the region where slavery was most common before 1865. In some districts there are many more black than white people, but in general they are in the minority, even in the south.

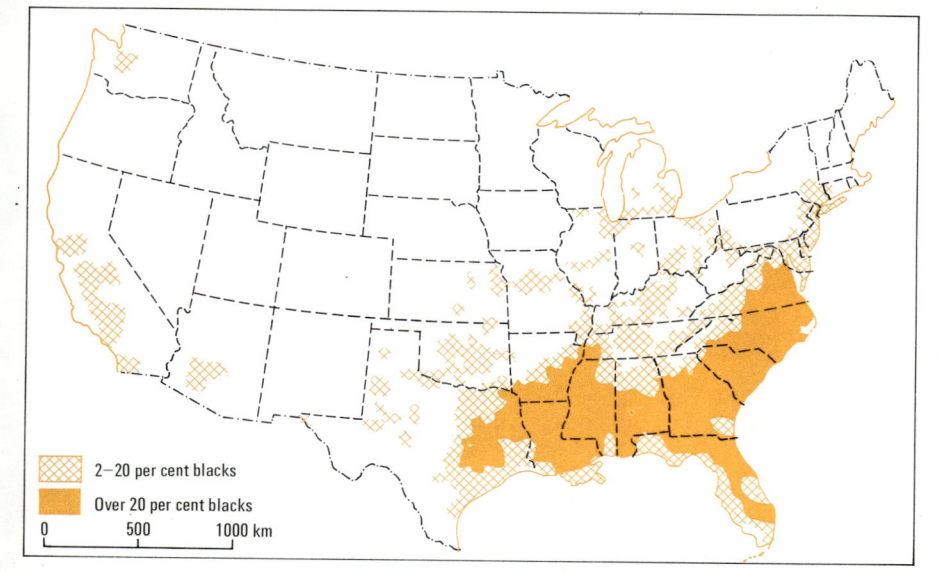

Unlike China and the U.S.S.R., where the minority people settled mainly in the

poorer lands (except for the Ukraine), in the U.S.A. it was only the Indians who were pushed out of the best areas. The land in the south-eastern states is generally fertile and could be very prosperous. The black people and some poor whites do not get the benefit from this, since the land and other property, and the factories, nearly always belong to large white landholders.

Language

The language of the U.S.A. is English although many other languages are spoken. Spanish is often heard in the Mexican border states, and other European languages are spoken in isolated 'pockets' here and there. The blacks have almost completely lost their original African languages and they speak English. There are, of course, quite big differences in accent, particularly between the southern and northern states. Many words and phrases which first came from America have been adopted into the English language.

Religion

There is no 'established' church or 'Church of America' as there is a 'Church of England', and the government does nothing to support any one particular church, although the various forms of Christianity are the most common religions in the U.S.A. There are many Americans who have no religious belief. Of those who do belong to a church (more than half the total population), somewhere between 30 and 50 million are Roman Catholics. About one in every seven persons in the U.S.A. is a Catholic. However, if all the 'Protestant' churches, such as Baptist, Methodist, Lutheran, and Episcopal (the Church of England in the United States), are taken together, they outnumber the Catholics. There are more than a hundred different types of Christian church in the U.S.A., quite apart from other religions.

Photo. 84 Baptism in the New World Church, one of the many fringe religions in the U.S.A.

Photo. 85 American Indians demonstrating for land rights in Washington. The native Americans claim that their forefathers were cheated of land by the European settlers who flooded across the continent in the ninteenth century

Discrimination against Minority Groups

With the exception of the Ukrainians in Russia, and the American blacks, most minority groups live in the poorer regions of their countries. In terms of wealth, influence, and standard of living, the United States blacks are usually at a disadvantage when compared with the whites. Even if they live in a pleasant part of the country, few of them own land as the people of European origin do. When you think about the differences in the opportunities available to whites and blacks, you will begin to understand why there are often problems in countries with minority groups. One factor involved here is fear. What do you think the majority of Americans might be frightened of? What changes do black Americans want?

See what you can find out about the Jewish people in the U.S.S.R. They are a minority, and their history there is one of persecution and discrimination. Many have had to leave their homes to settle in other countries. In America, Jewish people do not suffer in the same way, and are free to live, work, and practise their religion wherever they wish. With your teacher, compare and discuss the attitude of the majority of people in Russia and America to the Jewish minority.

There is a big difference in the location of ethnic groups in the three giant powers. In the U.S.S.R. and in China, there are a number of separate nationalities, living in their own parts of the country, with culture and traditions of their own. In the United States, minority

Photo. 86 A black American proudly proclaims his colour

groups are to be found living side by side, even in one city. In New York there are Chinese, Jewish, Italian, Afro-American, and other distinct communities. Chicago has a big Polish community. These people stay together, preserving their ethnic traditions and ways of life, even though they no longer live in the land of their ancestors. They may think of themselves as belonging to two separate national groups: they may be Chinese Americans, Polish Americans, Jewish Americans, Black Americans; and they can be proud of being both.

When the majority rejects the traditions of the minority group, as the Russians have done of the Jews, and the Americans of the African and Indian minorities, then there is resentment and trouble.

Assignments

1. Collect photographs and information about the various minority groups of the U.S.S.R. and China. Find out what you can about their languages and customs.

Using an atlas map of the U.S.A. pick out names which could be French, Spanish, or American Indian in origin.

2. Find out, from a reference book or encyclopaedia, the basic beliefs of the world's main religions, and the major divisions of belief within Christianity (e.g., the Orthodox Church, Roman Catholicism, and Protestantism). Discuss with your friends and teacher whether any government should openly support or oppose some particular religion or all religions in general. Should the Church have any special say in how a country is governed? (e.g., in England a Bishop in the Church of England is a member of the House of Lords and the Queen is regarded as head of both Church and State.)

3. Find out what American blacks are doing to build up pride in their Afro-American culture.

Photo. 87   A privately-owned farm in North Dakota

Photo. 88   The headquarter buildings of a Soviet collective farm

6 Farming Communities

In the U.S.A. farms are run along capitalist, profit-making lines. The farmer may own his own land, or rent it from a landlord, or the farm may often belong to a company. There is a great deal of variety. Some farms may be quite small, owned by one man and worked by him and his family. Others may be very large indeed with hundreds of workers employed by the owning company.

In the U.S.S.R., most farms are state owned. They may be run by a manager who is employed by the government, or if they are collective farms, they are run along **co-operative** lines. On a collective farm, the people work in teams or brigades, and they elect their own managers and have a committee which makes most of the important decisions, such as what crops to grow, what machinery to buy, and how work shall be allocated to the various teams. The farm has to give a large amount of the total crop each year to the state, but if the harvest is good and there is a lot left over, the people can use this for themselves, or the committee may decide to sell to make a cash profit. On a state farm the workers are paid wages, just as if they worked in a factory; on a collective their income varies to some extent according to the harvest. In addition to the state-owned land, the people are allowed to have small plots of their own on which they can grow crops for sale or for their own food, doing the necessary work in their spare time.

Photo 89   A Russian farmer near Odessa cultivates fruit for the use of his family

Photo. 90 A production brigade in north China breaks from work to study the words of Chairman Mao

In China the people all over the country are grouped into communes. These are often very large areas of land with many thousands of people, some living in small towns, some in villages, some on scattered farms. The commune has a council which makes the important decisions for the whole group, and this council works with the central government planners. The council can appeal to the government for help if necessary, and may ask for expert advisers to visit the commune. Under the commune council the people are grouped into **production brigades**, each brigade containing about a hundred families. The area worked by one brigade varies enor-

Photo. 91 Machinery workshop on a Chinese farm

mously depending on the fertility of the soil and the ease with which it can be worked. Land in China is very scarce, and a whole family might live off an area not larger than a suburban backyard in England. The brigade owns its own farming tools and animals, and the land. Each brigade is divided again into small teams of twenty or thirty families; each family receives a basic allowance of pay and goods, but a strict record is kept of the work done and extra rewards go to those who have worked best.

On the pages following there are maps and some photographs of privately-owned farms, collective farms and communes. The types of crop grown are different in each case, and this explains some of the contrasts: a different farm organization is required to grow cotton than to grow wheat; rice production is different again. However, other differences have very little to do with crops, relating more to political control, ownership and organization.

Photo. 92 Members of a brigade cultivate between rows of wheat. With so many workers, expensive labour-saving machines are not needed

Fig. 18 Positions of communes near Sian and Canton

Fig. 19 (right) Sinjao commune

Chinese communes
Sinjao, near Canton

Sinjao commune is an island group in the delta region of the Si-Kiang river south-east of Canton city. The position of the commune is shown in Fig. 18 and the ways in which the land is used are mapped in Fig. 19. Canton is one of China's largest cities, with a population of well over three million people; the fact that the commune is so close largely decides what crops shall be grown. Some food crops like wheat grain and rice can be transported long distances in trains or trucks without suffering, but others are perishable and do not travel well. These must be grown as close as possible to the places where they will be used. The map shows that the most important crops in Sinjao commune are of this kind: fruit and vegetables.

The total number of people living in this commune is about 50 000; there are over 11 000 families. Their houses are closely grouped into villages, as marked on the map. As far as possible the villages are built on ground that is slightly higher than the rest. The whole of Sinjao is an island. The land is very low and flat so that in the high river seasons (after the monsoon rains), there is great danger of flooding. The fields are protected by earthen banks and dykes. In the dry season, however, this low situation is helpful since it enables water to be taken easily from the river to be used to irrigate the crops.

The fruits grown include lychees, peaches, and bananas. The trees stand usually on the earth banks which are about five metres wide with ditches two or three metres deep between. The fruit trees need plenty of water, but they die if their roots are surrounded by water-logged soil. Pineapples are also grown in rows, in low bushy clumps of spiny leaves. Vegetables grown include cabbages of many different types, beans, and onions. These, too, grow on narrow strips of land between ditches; the ditches drain the land during the wet season and are used for irrigation in the dry season. Multi-cropping is the rule; as soon as one harvest is taken another crop is planted in the same soil. Sometimes as many as eight harvests are possible in one year.

The climate graph for Canton (page 51) shows that high temperatures prevail in all seasons, so providing there is sufficient water, plant growth never ceases. To take so many crops from the land is unusual and can lead to loss of fertility in the soil. Some of the commune workers have the never-ending task of dredging up mud and silt from the river bed to spread on the land to keep it in good condition. They use flat-bottomed boats for this purpose, scraping up the mud and dumping it into the boat, then rowing or poling it via the river channels and ditches to the part of the commune where it is needed. The sewage of the city of Canton itself is another important source of fertilizers.

Rice growing in Sinjao is similar to rice production in other areas of China (see photos). Usually two crops each year can be obtained, with sometimes a vegetable crop between the harvesting of the first rice, and planting of the second. A production brigade in Sinjao has about forty workers, both men and women, who work eight hours a day for six days a week. At busy times, as during the rice planting, they are likely to work longer hours.

Other work done by the commune includes some fishing, and pig keeping, and there are some dairy cattle to provide fresh milk for the city. These animals are kept most of the time in stalls, being fed with rice straw, grass mowings, and some 'cattle cake' from factories in Canton. There are also some small industries, such as fruit preserving, boat building, and making farm machinery. Some of the young women do embroidery and dress making. Their products go to shops in Canton for sale to foreign visitors. The commune has its own primary schools; all children have to attend schools where they learn to read and write though few go on to secondary school. The commune also has its own hospitals, although the serious cases go to the city for treatment.

The way of life in this commune is greatly affected by the nearby city; the crops grown, the education and medical services available, are different from other communes which are further from Canton. In these, rice is often almost the only crop; fruit, vegetable and milk production is carried on only in a small way to satisfy the needs of the local people.

Photo. 93 A woman in Canton carries sugar cane grown on her commune to sell in the city

Photo. 94 Picking cabbages for market

Photos. 95–105 In China rice is an even more important crop than wheat. The map (Fig. 28) shows the area where rice is the major crop. As these very old pictures show, in some cases the ancient and modern methods of rice growing are still exactly the same. In some areas, machinery has recently been introduced

95 and 96 Ploughing the fields with water-buffalo. This is followed by fertilizing the soil, and planting the seeds

97 and 98 Seedlings are transplanted by hand. In some areas a simple machine is used to deposit rows of about 12 plants at a time

99 Water wheels worked by treadmills are still used to flood the fields

100 The rows of rice plants are cultivated to remove weeds. Compare this picture with Photo. 91, page 71

101 The rice is harvested with hand sickles. Some communes have machines now to help with this job. The stalks are then threshed to separate the grain from the straw, as in drawing 102. The rice is spread to dry, 103.

104 and 105 : Winnowing. The grain is separated from the chaff as it falls through the basket-like sieve

100

101 割穀

102 臨殻

103

104 飄穀

105

Photo. 106 Oxen are used to plough the hillside terraces

Fig. 20 A commune near Sian in Shensi

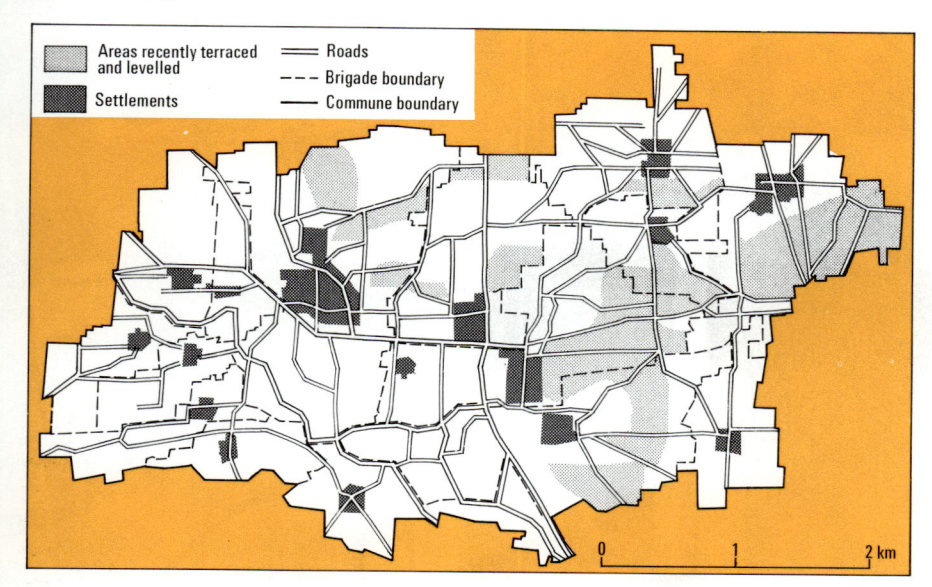

Areas recently terraced and levelled
Settlements
Roads
Brigade boundary
Commune boundary

0   1   2 km

A Commune in Shensi

Fig. 20 shows a commune in Shensi, south of the city of Sian. Compared with the Sinjao commune, the land is higher, and there is no major river. The part of the commune to the east is hilly, with light, fertile soil known as **loess**. This is a deposit of dust blown from the desert lands of the west, built up over many thousands of years into layers hundreds of metres deep over large regions of northern China. To provide flat spaces for crops in these hills of dusty material it is necessary to bank the slopes up into a series of terraces. The areas where this has been done are marked on the commune map. Photos show the resulting 'stepped' appearance of the land.

The western part of this commune is lower and flatter. This area of China, as the climate map shows, has a low rainfall. The flat land is covered by a network of irrigation ditches. The water is pumped to the surface from over 200 wells, and enough water is found in this way to supply about one third of the region.

The main crop is wheat. The commune owns 34 threshing machines, a harvester, and 42 ploughing machines. These are usually pulled by animals. Large amounts of chemical fertilizer are used. Other crops include vegetables, and there are many pigs and cattle. The commune also has some small industries, repair shops for machinery, wood-working workshops to make carts and repair them, brickworks for house building, and of course there are mills and bakeries, which take some of the wheat crop for local use.

The total population is about 16 000, smaller than Sinjao commune, and further from any large city. There are 16 brigades, all of about the same size. The commune map shows how the land is divided up between these brigades. On the flatter land, a brigade can work quite a large area, but on the difficult, terraced slopes, each brigade is expected to work a smaller area.

The settlements are grouped or 'nucleated', and the district has its own schools and hospitals.

Photo. 107 Terraced loess soils in China

Fig. 21 Positions of the Budenny collective, and of a state farm near Atbasar

Fig. 22 Budenny collective farm

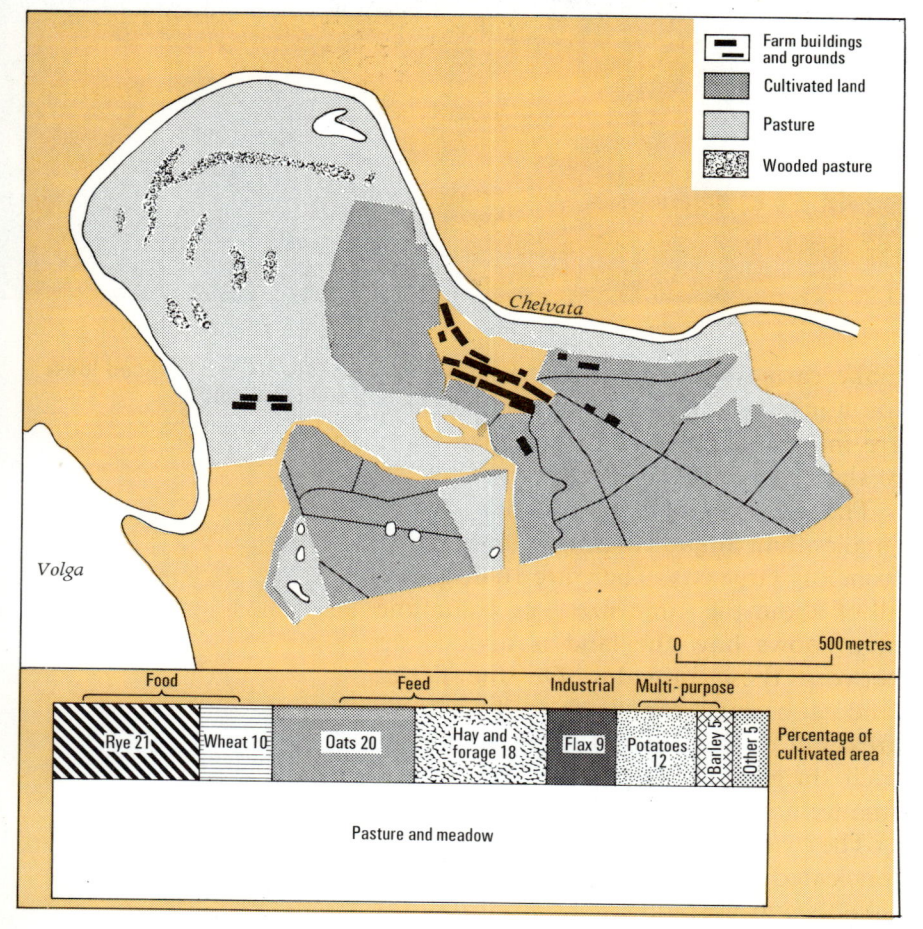

Farming in Russia
The Budenny collective

The Budenny collective farm, shown in Fig. 22, is on the Volga River about 400 km north-east of Moscow and 120 km north of the town of Gorki. On this collective there are about sixty families. Compared with some others it is quite small, and a few years ago it was joined to several other similar farms and made into one larger collective. However, in most ways it is still worked as one unit.

This region of the Russian Soviet has a long, cold winter with snow cover for more than four months, and the Volga is frozen for a similar period. It is outside the main grain growing regions of the U.S.S.R. The diagram (Fig. 22) shows the main crops; more than half the land is pasture and meadow for cattle. Feeding the cattle in winter requires large quantities of fodder; the rye, wheat and oats are grown for this, and are often harvested while still green. Hay and other forage crops are grown. The cattle are kept in stalls during the cold season.

Flax is grown for the long linen fibres of its stems, which are spun and woven into cloth in the town of Kostroma, a

Photo. 108 Workers' houses on a collective farm in Kazakhstan. Note electric power supplies and television aerials on most houses. (Other pictures of Russian farming can be seen on p. 86)

Fig. 23 State farm near Atbasar in North Kazakhstan

centre of the linen industry about 150 km higher up the river. Potatoes are also used there for making starch and glucose.

The buildings of the farm, and most of the cultivation, are on slightly higher ground than the pasture which lies mainly inside the loop of the Chelvata River. In spring, when the snow melts, there is often flooding of large areas on the lower ground. There are some areas of this low land which are never fully drained. They are remains of former river channels, for the Chelvata in the past has changed its course on many occasions, sometimes leaving behind long, narrow lakes, called ox-bows, which have silted up slowly and now are still damp, with scattered trees, usable as pasture only during the summer. Some ox bows are shown on the map, still full of water.

A state farm near Atbasar

The farm in Fig. 23 is a state farm (the difference between state farms and collectives is explained on page 69). It lies near the town of Atbasar. Snow cover in this area usually lasts about five months, but the summers are quite hot. The soil is mainly very fertile 'black earth', and the most important crop is wheat. The maps show the areas which have been cultivated recently for the first time, as new land is taken in, and some other areas are marked out for later ploughing. The grain from this farm is loaded onto railway trucks and carried for storage at Atbasar. Most of the towns in this region are concerned with the use of farm produce; milling and meat packing, and leather tanning. The railways of the area are used both to carry the farm products into the towns, and to take the processed food (flour, canned meat, etc.) to the much larger cities of the rest of the U.S.S.R. To the north-west the industrial cities of Magnitogorsk and Sverdlovsk take much of the farm produce of the Atbasar region.

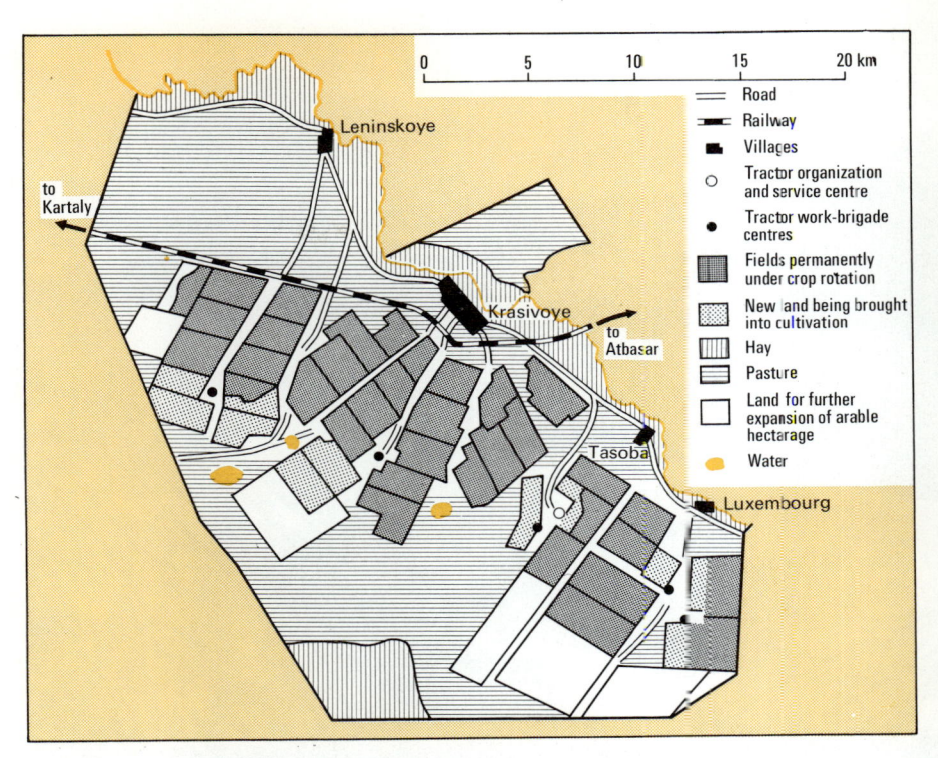

Photo. 109 Two combine-harvesters work together to bring in the wheat. Much of the U.S. farmer's wealth is invested in farm equipment. Compare the style of farming shown here with that seen in the photographs of China

Farming in the U.S.A.
A wheat farm in Montana

The farm in Fig. 25 is privately owned, belonging to the Holtz family. It lies 18 km north of the small town of Great Falls, in Montana, U.S.A. The farmer, Mr. Holtz, and his son, do most of the work between them except during early summer and the harvest season, when a few extra men are hired to help, one to drive a combine harvester and two others to drive trucks to take the grain from the harvesters to the store. To enable such a small work force to operate the entire farm, almost everything has to be done by machinery; there are two tractors, three combine harvesters, a seed drill and a crop spraying machine, two trucks for grain, and a number of different cultivating machines, including harrows, and weeders. There is also a snow plough, several other old trucks for odd jobs, and the family owns a jeep and two cars. A small aeroplane, flown by Mr. Holtz's son, may be used for crop spraying, but is mainly for travel and recreation.

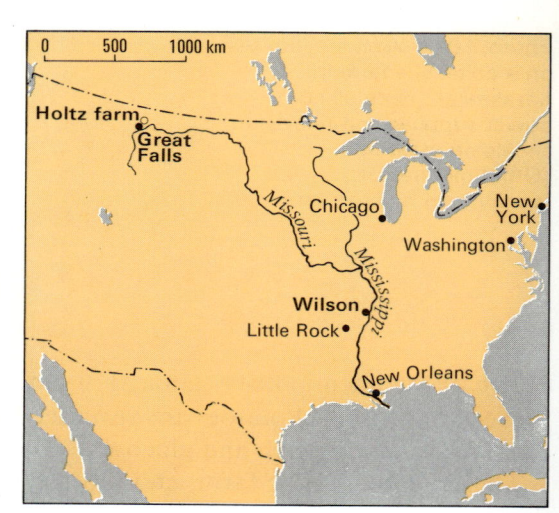

The map on p. 44 shows that this area can expect over two months of snow cover during the year. The working year begins in April with planting of barley

Fig. 24 Position of a wheat farm near Great Falls, and of the farming town of Wilson

Farmstead

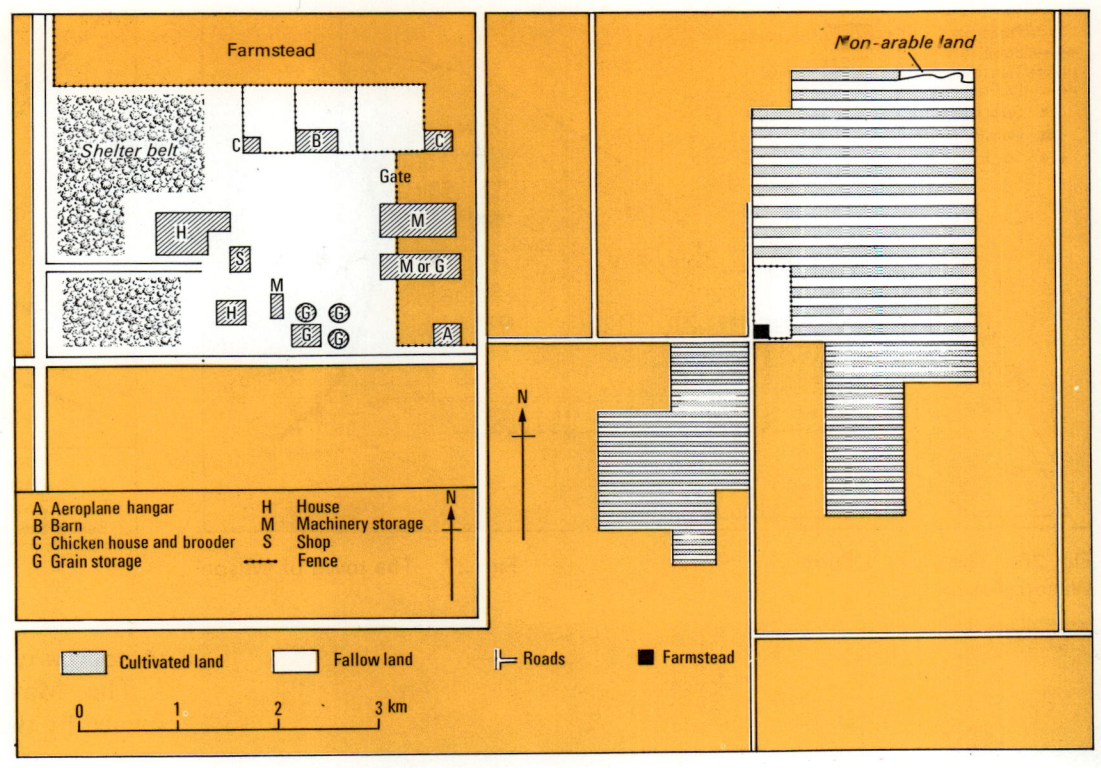

A Aeroplane hangar
B Barn
C Chicken house and brooder
G Grain storage
H House
M Machinery storage
S Shop
----- Fence

Cultivated land | Fallow land | Roads | Farmstead

0   1   2   3 km

Non-arable land

Fig. 25 The Holtz family wheat farm, with detailed plan of the farmstead (inset)

and of spring wheat (see p. 86). The land on the farm is divided into narrow strips, and the grain is planted on alternate sections with the others left fallow. The fallow land has time to recover from the previous year's use, and it is frequently cleared of weeds. The reason for strip farming in this way is to prevent the light soil being blown away by wind. If a large area of soil were left exposed without crops on it, there would be serious losses every year and the region might quickly become a desert-like dust bowl. 'Wind-break' trees are planted to help prevent soil being blown.

After planting, as the young crops grow, the weeding of the fallow strips continues by machine, and aerial spraying follows in June to kill those weeds that have appeared among the crop. The wheat harvest is in August, and the barley soon afterwards, after which the winter wheat is planted in the un-cropped strips. The land is not ploughed because this would break up the surface, encouraging wind erosion, and would also allow the soil to dry too much. The land is merely harrowed before seeding. The average rainfall is under 300 mm per year. The harvest of the wheat takes about ten days, and the grain is stored on the farm in steel silos until it is hauled by truck to the huge grain storages at the railway, in January.

Fig. 26 The Mary V Farm, Wilson, Arkansas

Fig. 27 The town of Wilson

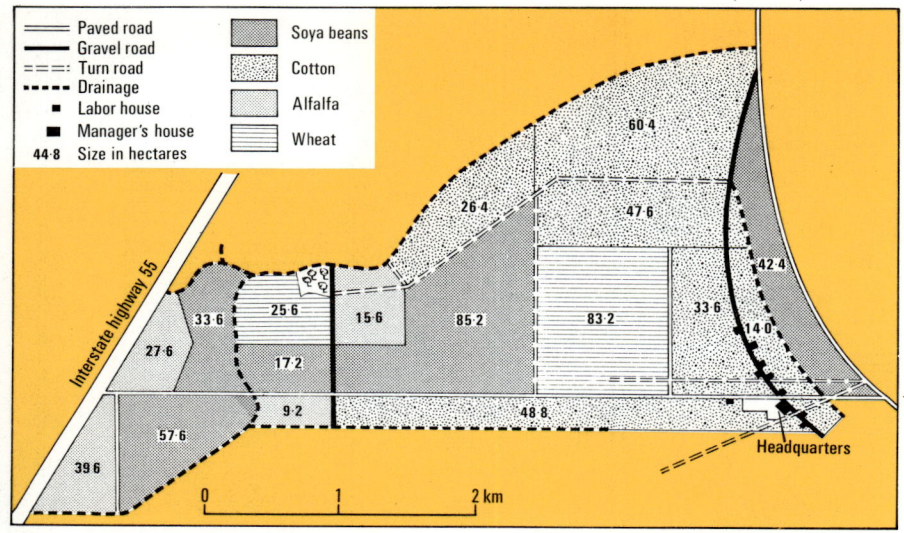

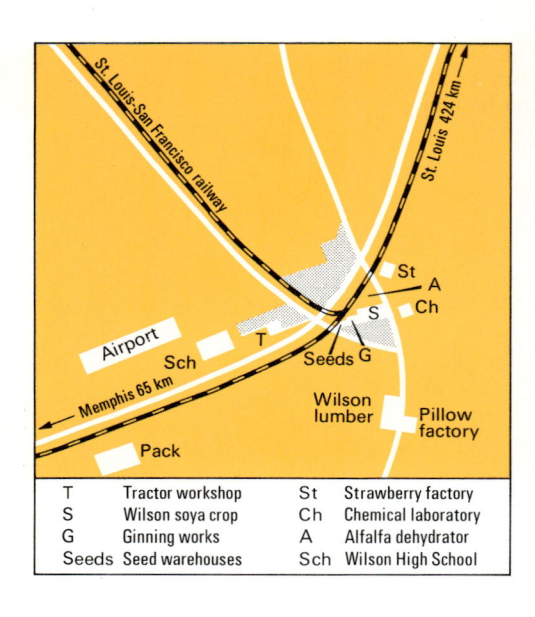

A company farm in Arkansas

The Mary V Farm in Arkansas is owned by the Wilson company. The company owns 22 farms altogether in the district around the town of Wilson in Arkansas, close to the Mississippi River in Southern U.S.A. Each farm is run by a manager working for a fixed salary, and the farm workers are employed and paid by the company. Profit from the farm goes to the company, which also has to pay for any machinery required, and has to meet all the other costs, or 'overheads', from the sale of the produce.

The farm plan shows the crops grown. Soya beans are very important in Arkansas;

Photo. 110 Bulk carriers load grain on the Mississippi River at New Orleans

the oil pressed from the beans is used in margarine and salad dressings; the meal left after pressing is used for cattle and chicken feed. Alfalfa (see Fig. 26) is known as lucerne in Europe; it is a feed crop for animals, and also is planted on land that has previously been used for cotton. Cotton draws a great deal from the soil; lucerne and beans are both crops that restore fertility to the land since they 'fix' nitrogen from the air and restore it to the soil. The nitrogen salts accumulate in the roots of these plants and remain behind when the beans and lucerne are taken. Some wheat is grown; this is all winter wheat. The winters in Arkansas are relatively mild; usually only a week or two of snow cover (see Fig. 7).

Photo. 11 The Mary V Farm

Photo. 112 Picking cotton by hand in southern U.S.A. Black labour is still used for this exhausting work, although many farms have big cotton-picking machines. Cotton is grown in all three of the giants. It is grown to provide raw material for manufacture into cotton cloth and other products

The largest single crop is cotton, and as explained above, this is grown in rotation with beans and alfalfa. To protect the cotton from pests, especially the **boll weevil**, an insect that feeds on the unripe cotton 'boll', the farm employs aerial crop sprayers who spread insecticides over the growing crop once a week during the growing season. When the bolls are nearly ready to open, the aeroplanes may also spray a substance that causes them all to ripen at the same time. When the bolls are ripe they burst open, each plant carrying numerous fluffy balls of cotton, and the cotton picking machines go in. The raw cotton contains many seeds which are separated from the soft white **lint** in a cotton gin.

The Wilson company owns the cotton gin which processes the cotton from all the 22 farms, and in the town there are also company plants for pressing soya beans, drying alfalfa, making the chemical sprays, and repairing tractors and other machines. The town also has an airstrip, a school, and a timber works. The company owns 180 tractors and the farm managers are provided with two-way radios in their cars so they can keep in touch with the company headquarters, and call quickly if assistance is needed.

A constant danger to the whole of this region is flooding from the Mississippi. The land of the farm lies below the river embankments or **levees**, which are 15 metres high. To drain the fields there are many ditches and pumps, but a breach in the levees higher up stream could destroy all the farms owned by the company, and the town as well. Disastrous floods have occurred many times in the history of the Mississippi valley.

Assignments

1. Each farm and commune map is provided with a scale. Use this to estimate and compare the size of each. (Remember that the Arkansas farm is one of 22 owned by the company).

2. A company farm has a manager, and so has a state farm in the U.S.S.R. Discuss with your friends what differences there would be between managing a state farm and a company farm. Compare the problems of the two different managers with (a) those of a private-owner-farmer, and (b) those facing the elected management committee of a commune.

3. Count the number of villages on each of the Chinese communes. How does the distribution of villages in these communes compare with that on the Soviet Collectives and the American company farm?

4. What reasons are there for the lack of machinery on the Chinese communes?

Photo. 113 Cotton requires a warm climate with a long season free from cold weather or frost. The maps (Fig. 28) show the main areas where cotton is grown. The plants require fertile soil and large amounts of water. If there is not enough water from natural rainfall, the cotton fields must be irrigated. In the U.S.S.R. cotton is usually grown under irrigation These cotton-picking machines are operating on a collective farm in Azerbaijan

Photo. 114 A production brigade in China picks cotton and spreads it to dry in the sun

85

Photo. 115 Rice harvesting in the Ukrainian Republic. Compare this mechanized farming with that shown in Photo. 101

Photo. 116 Wheat harvesting on a state farm in the U.S.S.R. Machinery is similar to that shown in Photo. 109

Crops

Three maps (Fig. 28b) show areas of China, the U.S.S.R. and the U.S.A. where wheat is grown. Wheat is not the only important crop of these regions; often it is grown alongside other grain crops, such as rye or barley, and frequently there are root crops also, such as potatoes and beet. However, the maps show that wheat is grown over very large areas in all three of the giant powers, and it is one of the most important crops.

In each case there are two distinct types of wheat, 'winter wheat' and 'spring wheat'. Winter wheat is planted in the early part of the winter and the seed grain lies in the ground through the coldest season so that it is already beginning to grow when the warmer weather comes. Spring wheat is sown in spring, and can therefore only begin to grow during the spring and summer. Both types of wheat must be harvested before the cold weather returns again.

The photographs (pp. 71, 80, 86) show wheat farming in progress. Although the work takes place at different seasons, the process is very much the same for the winter and spring sown types. The land must be prepared for the seed, by ploughing and harrowing, then the sowing follows. Severe frost or storm damage during the growing period is always a danger, but all being well the harvest takes place in the late summer or during the autumn. The crop has to be cut, and the heads of wheat threshed to separate the grains. The grain then has to be milled to produce flour.

There are important differences shown in the photographs, between the ways this essential work is done in the three countries. As time goes on, it may be expected that these differences will become less, although they may never disappear completely because of the greater proportion of Chinese people to land area. Chinese agriculture will probably always be **labour-intensive**; great numbers of people, rather than expensive machinery, will be used to do the work.

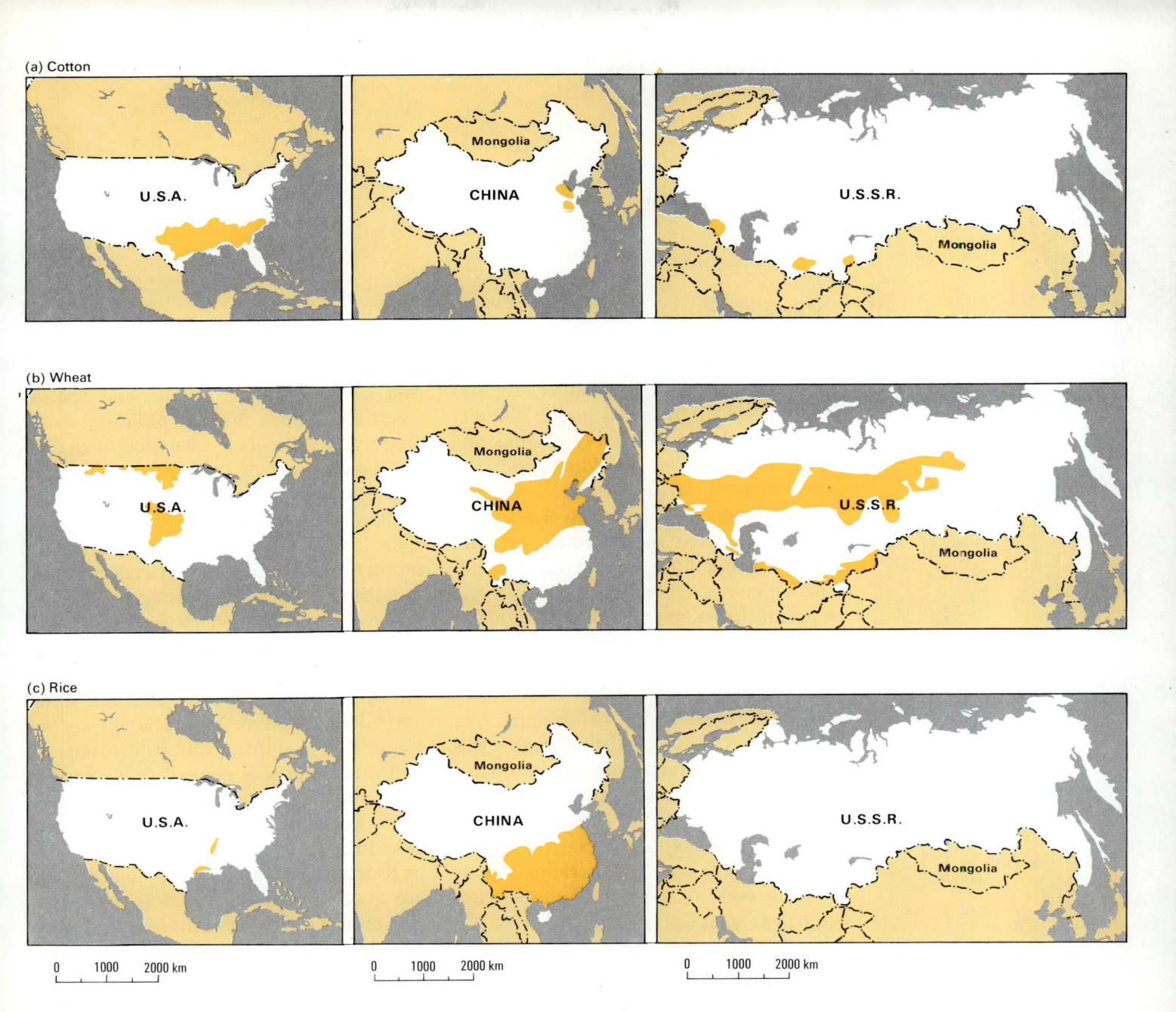

Fig. 28 Cotton, wheat, and rice growing regions

7 Industries

Heavy industries are concerned with mining, drilling, and quarrying for raw materials (metal ores, coal, oils, etc.), and with turning these into products such as metals, plastics, fuel, and power. Closely related to these are heavy engineering works, such as shipbuilding and the production of large machines, engines and armaments. There must be special plants for rolling metals into bars and sheets, casting and forging metals into machine components, and forming metal or plastic tubes, pipes, and wires, all of which are needed by other industries.

Medium and light industries produce consumer goods (i.e., goods which may be bought from shops or dealers). An item such as a radio, for example, will use copper and aluminium, plastics, steel screws and bolts, glass, paints and many other substances. All of these are manufactured in other factories and works before being taken to the radio manufacturing concern. Vehicles such as cars and heavy trucks or tractors are built mainly from steel; components needed include sheet steel for body work, forgings and casting for the engine and special steels for springs. Vehicle building works frequently have their own steel furnaces, but a motor car or truck is very complex and many of its parts will be made of materials that come from other industries: there are electric lights, generators and motors, glass and plastic parts, switches, handles and locks, upholstery, tyres and brakes, parts plated with chromium, special paints and finishes.

As well as manufacturing, there are the industries which process food and other agricultural produce and pack it in various ways. For example, fruit from orchards and greenhouses is cooked or made into juice and then canned, or fermented to make wine; grain is milled into flour and baked into bread and cake; cotton, wool, or flaxen fibres, as well as synthetic fibres, are spun and woven into cloth and made into clothing; timber from forests is sawn into lumber for furniture or building, or pulped to make paper.

Bricks, steel, concrete, and cement as well as timber provide materials for the

Photo. 117 Workmen repair a high voltage power line near Shanghai. Would such work be very different in the U.S.A. or U.S.S.R.? What crop is grown in the fields below?

building industry. Power for all these industries and for domestic use is produced by burning coal, gas, or oil, to drive generators. Nuclear power stations and hydro-electric schemes are other great sources of energy.

In addition to processing, manufacturing, and power there are millions of people engaged in **service industries** such as transport, sales, repairing and maintaining buildings and machines, publishing, health, banking, entertaining, and teaching.

Modern industry is thus very complicated, and while there are important differences between the three giant powers in terms of their development, the work actually done in the various industries is very much the same wherever it is. Steel, for example, is made in the same ways in China as it is in the U.S.S.R. and U.S.A., and the Chinese worker in the steel plant at Anshan in Manchuria, for instance, is likely to understand far more about the jobs done by steelworkers in other places than he does about the work of Chinese in other types of industry. In the same way, although there may be differences in size and appearance, the processes involved in building a car, making paper, or building a block of flats, are very similar wherever they are carried on.

A nation which has all its industries well advanced is often called a **developed** nation; this term accurately describes the U.S.A., where industries of every imaginable kind are found. The U.S.S.R. is developing very rapidly. After the Revolution the communist government launched a great drive for more heavy industry; there was a series of **five year plans** (see p. 21); people were taken off the farm lands and given jobs in mines and factories, and geologists were sent all over the country in search of new sources of coal, iron, oil, and other essential minerals. It was necessary to build up the heavy industries first, but now after more than fifty years the U.S.S.R. has made enormous progress in every direction.

Photo. 118 Packing cans of meat in a Shanghai food processing plant. Why do you suppose the packing crate has some English labels?

89

The Great Leap Forward

During the period from 1957 to 1961, the Chinese leaders felt that China's industries were not making fast enough progress. They had accepted help from the U.S.S.R.; engineers and industrial experts from the Soviet Union came to train Chinese workers in new skills, and large new machines, built in the U.S.S.R., were imported and set up. However, all the new factories were on the European model, and it was difficult for Chinese workers, who in many cases had never even seen a modern factory or steel plant, to learn how to operate the machines. Some of the new plants were finished and ready to begin work when it was realized that there were no raw materials for them, or no power supply, and sometimes when work did begin there were no clear instructions about what kind of product was needed or where it was to go.

The government decided that in China, where there was very little established industry, and no general knowledge of machines, western methods should be abandoned. Instead, since there were so many people, a lot of the jobs done by machines in modern factories should be done by hand. This nation-wide use of labour-intensive methods was planned to advance China in one great industrial leap forward. To increase steel production, older people in the villages were asked if they could remember any old mine shafts in their district, or whether they had heard stories about small iron works in the past. When such old mines were found, they were re-opened. Crude furnaces were built of local bricks and fired by coal if any was found locally. Soon there were sixty million people working at such small, backyard furnaces, producing crude iron. Unfortunately, in such home-made furnaces the iron produced was usually of very poor quality, and the workers, without any scientific knowledge or method of improving their product, were often wasting their time. One American who was living and working in China at this time, wrote the following:

'We dropped everything else and built brick chimneys in the factory yard. Radiators, pots and pans and every bit of available scrap went into the ovens, and peasants from the countryside poured in to help. The whole place was raving mad. Furnaces were glowing everywhere, and at night the city glowed red. The street lights had gone off to save electricity, and the bulbs in the houses were a kind of dim yellow. People, machines, everything was being strained to the limit and cracking up. Workers who had to tend furnaces at night

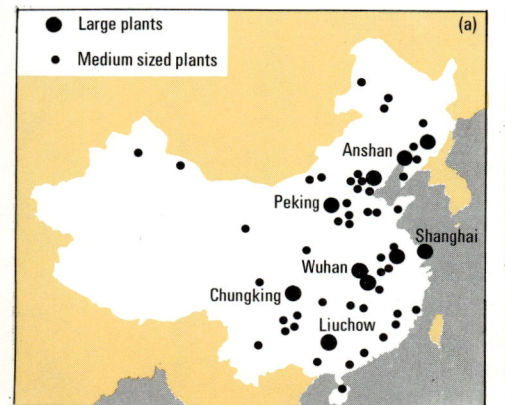

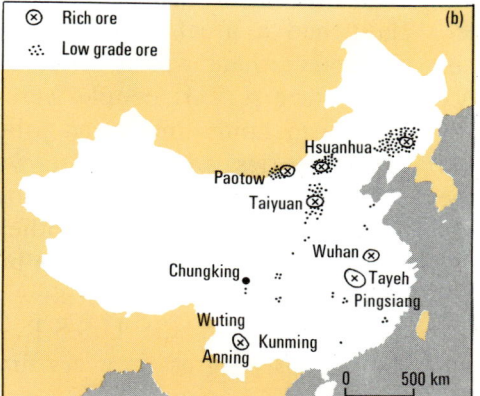

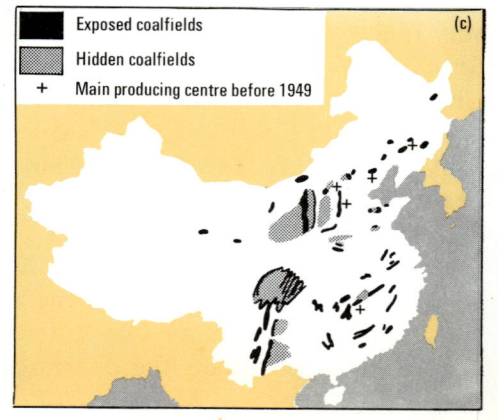

Fig. 29 The Chinese steel industry: (a) steel production plants; (b) iron deposits; (c) coalfields

and go to the factory by day were having all sorts of accidents ... at first the people were really carried away. They felt proud that they could make iron. The trouble was, nothing human or mechanical could stand that terrible pace.' (*Saturday Evening Post* 16.11.63, p. 106)

In the middle of this frenzied effort, the Soviet Union withdrew all the help that had been given, the advisers left China, and in some cases the factories they had started to build were left unfinished. On top of this blow, a severe drought destroyed crops over large parts of the country in 1959, 1960, and 1961. Many of the large modern factories came to a complete standstill as the machines broke down, and much of the poor iron from the backyard furnaces was good only for the scrapheap. Hunger and disease increased. The great leap forward came to a sad end in 1961, with Chinese industry temporarily disrupted. Since then China has built up some industries along modern lines, without help from the U.S.S.R., but also puts a lot of effort into small-scale, simply equipped factories which cost little to set up. Many people are needed to produce comparatively little, because there are few machines to help them, but in a poor, densely-populated country like China, this does not matter very much.

Steel

China

In China, industry is very much less developed than in either of the other giant powers. To mention just one example, when the government took control in 1949, there was only one large steelworks in the whole country, and that was in ruins. Compared with the U.S.S.R., China has had less than thirty years in which to develop industries, and in spite of five year plans and a period, beginning in 1958, called 'the great leap forward' (see p. 90), China still has far to go in developing industry.

From the maps (Fig. 29) it may be seen that the steel industry in China is concentrated in areas where both iron and coal are within reach.

One of the most important industrial enterprises in China is the Wuhan Iron and Steel Corporation. It runs eighteen factories which are sub-divided into 101 workshops. In 1966 it had 35 000 employees of whom 5000 were miners, 2300 technicians and engineers, 7000 administrators, and 5000 worked in service or welfare jobs. The last figure may seem large. These service jobs exist because in China, housing, medical treatment, nurseries, libraries, and canteens and other such amenities are provided by the employer rather than through a special

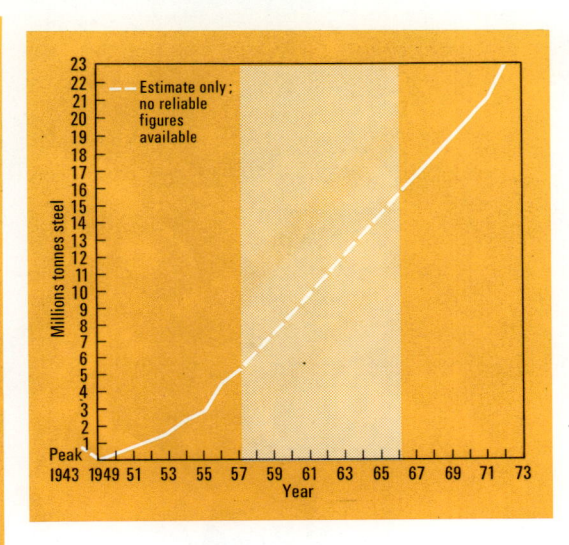

Fig. 30   Steel production in China from 1943

Photo. 119 Wuhan steelworkers wearing safety helmets, dark goggles, and heat-resistant gloves

government agency, so that factories must employ personnel for all these undertakings.

The Corporation runs plants and mines which satisfy its needs for coal, coke, iron ore, pig iron, various chemicals, and certain components. The products of this great industrial complex are very varied. It was set up with Soviet aid in the 1950s and absorbed many smaller enterprises already in existence. It represents an attempt to disperse industry, to take it closer to the sources of raw material and to develop the hinterland as a counterbalance to the far greater industrialization of the coastal area.

The Steel Industry

To make steel, iron ore is smelted in a blast furnace with some limestone and coke; the coke burns in a strong air blast blown in at the base of the furnace, the limestone acts as a flux, and allows the iron to separate from the impurities in the ore. The furnace, after burning for some time, contains rather impure molten iron which can then be drawn off at the bottom while more coke, iron, and lime is fed in above. The iron, either cast into 'pigs' or while still liquid, is then fed into a steel furnace where further purification takes place; the amount of carbon in the metal is adjusted, and small amounts of other metals such as tungsten, nickel, and manganese, may be added depending on the type of steel required. Most steel is of the simplest 'mild steel' type: iron combined with about eight parts in a hundred (8%) of carbon.

The chief raw materials for steelworks are coke, made from certain types of coal, and iron ore. Iron is a very common mineral and nearly all rock contains some. However, for use in a blast furnace, the iron-bearing rock must contain large proportions of iron. In the same way, not all coal is suitable for blast furnace coke; special coking coal is needed. So a successful steelworks needs to be within reach of good quality iron ore quarries, and coking-coal mines. It is usually not possible to find both together in the same area, so the works needs good railway or waterway transport links with iron and coal mines. Transport of the finished steel away from the works is equally vital.

Photo. 120 Operators of one of three small converters at the Anshan tube-casting mill

The Neighbourhood Factory

Neighbourhood factories are an important feature of Chinese industrialization. They require little capital and have often been set up by housewives with little or no government aid. For example, in 1958, the women of one Peking lane began to feel left out. Everyone was talking of their jobs, of the importance of working to build China until she caught up with the developed countries. So these women decided to set up a tailoring shop where they could make clothes for the families of other women who worked. With their first earnings they bought a sewing machine. None of them could have afforded such a thing before, they had always made everything by hand. They were very proud of this machine. Now they could work faster and make more money.

Over the years this shop has grown into a small garment factory with nearly 50 workers. It has a contract with a big department store, a nearby theatre orders costumes from it, and now it is going to start making protective clothing for a factory. Recently the women in the factory have decided to purchase button-making machinery, so a group of them will branch off into this associated industry. They have worked for years for wages which are low, even for a poor country, and they are very proud of what they have done.

Workshops like these are to be found all over China. They produce a great variety of things from cloth shoes to components for the electronics industry. For a country like China this sort of development can make a fairly significant, though comparatively minor, contribution to industrialization.

Photo. 121 Anshan steelworks

The largest steel plant in China is at Anshan, in Manchuria. The Anshan works was built originally by the Japanese before the Second World War, but the plant was virtually destroyed or dismantled at the end of the war, and the re-building was slow. A third steelworks was started at Paotow on the River Hoang Ho in Inner Mongolia, with two blast furnaces and four steel furnaces. These three steel plants account for most of China's modern steel industry, although as the map shows there are other small- and medium-sized plants in operation or being built in other regions. The Anshan plant is still by far the largest. Steel production in China is rising rapidly as the graph shows. There are other enterprises like these in China, but China cannot industrialize along these lines only, for she is too poor a country and cannot set up such expensive plants everywhere.

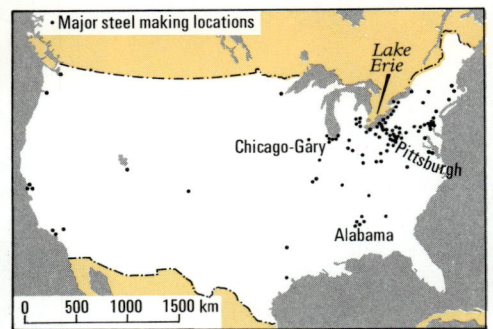

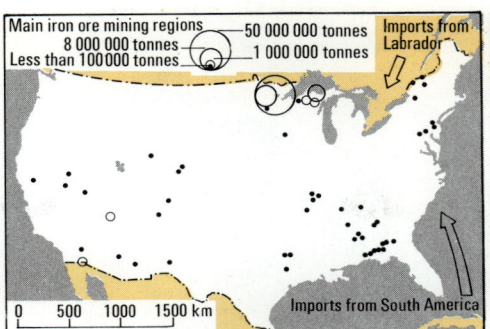

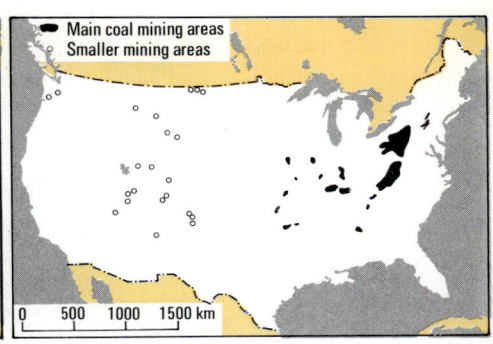

U.S.A.

The steel industry of the U.S.A. is far greater in size than that of China, and it is hardly possible to make a map showing every large or medium-sized steel plant. However, a map of the main areas where steel furnaces are operating (Fig. 31) shows that the industry is concentrated in the north-east, especially around Chicago and Gary, Pittsburgh, and the coast of Lake Erie. There are other important centres near the Atlantic coast and in Alabama, and smaller, but growing, centres in Texas, Colorado, and California. The main sources of coal and iron for the north-eastern industrial areas are shown in Fig. 31, and it is very important to notice that a great deal of the iron ore is imported to the U.S.A. from Canada, West Africa, and South America. The industry is so large that iron ores from nearby have been partly used up or 'worked out', and the furnaces must be fed from large, specially-constructed ore carriers which sail from Labrador down the St. Lawrence Seaway or down the Atlantic coast. Coal is in plentiful supply.

Fig. 31   The steel industry in the U.S.A.

Photo. 122   The end of a shift at the U.S.S. steelworks in Pittsburgh

Fig. 32   U.S. steel production from 1930

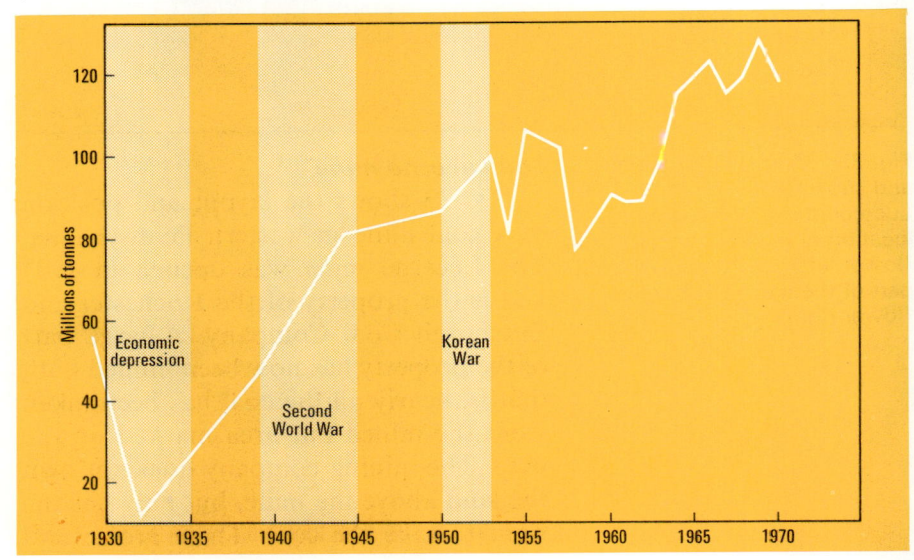

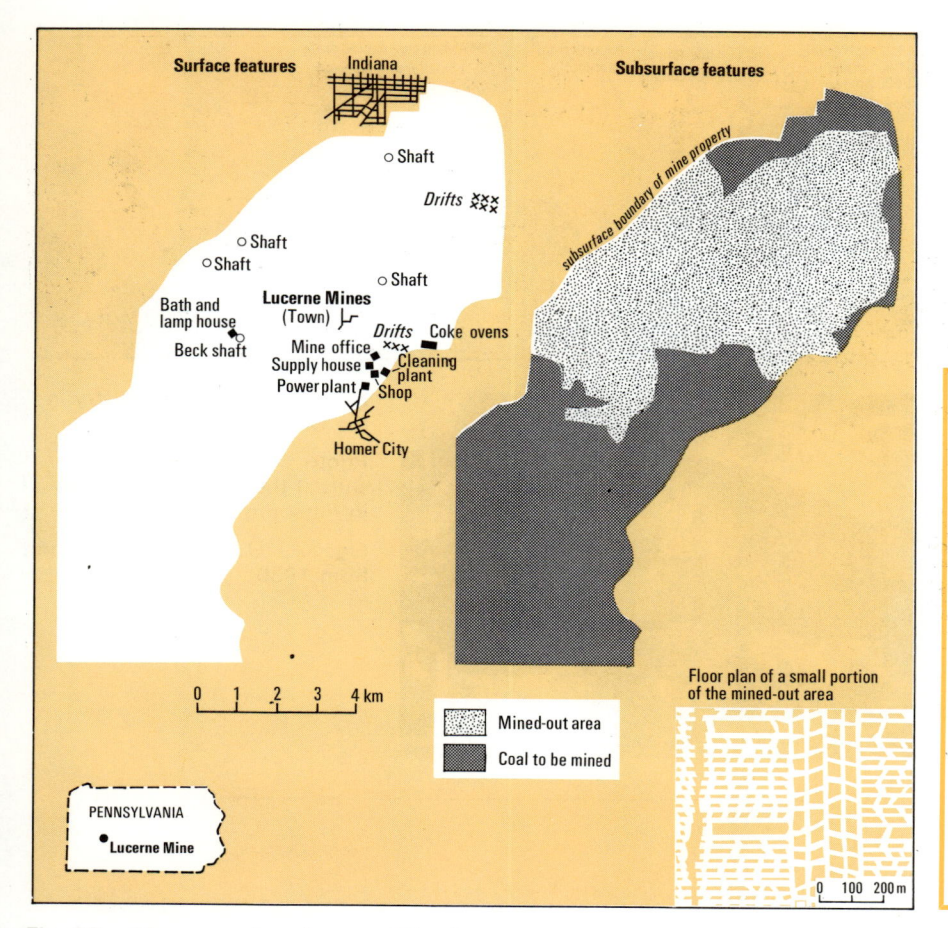

Fig. 33 Diagrams of surface and subsurface features of the Lucerne mine. Insets show location of mine in Pennsylvania (lower left), and a plan of a part of the mined-out area (lower right)

The Lucerne mine

Fig. 33 shows the layout and position of a coal mine in western Pennsylvania. The Lucerne mine was opened in 1907 and is the property of the Rochester and Pittsburgh Coal Company. A large part of the property has now been 'mined out', that is, nearly all the coal has been taken from the mined out area marked on the map. The mining company does not own the land above the mine, but only has the right to take the coal. There are several seams, but only the one called the Upper Freeport Seam is worked at present. The coal from this is of good quality and may be used to make coke for the Pittsburgh steel mills.

Altogether, the mine employs about 300 men, two hundred below ground and the rest on the surface. The mine has offices, a power plant, a bath house for the miners, supply and repair shops, all on the surface near the small towns of Homer and Lucerne Mines where many

'Open-pit' mining

Underground coal mining in the U.S.A. is now on the wane. In West Virginia, Kentucky, Ohio, Colorado, and Utah, huge earth-moving equipment is used to strip the top soil to get at the coal layers which are then lifted in giant scoops. This 'open-pit' mining leaves huge craters and scars on the landscape, so when areas are mined out they have to be refilled with earth. Tree plantings can then cover the former holes. Too often companies avoid the costly process of filling in and planting, so state and federal laws have been made to enforce this final constructive stage.

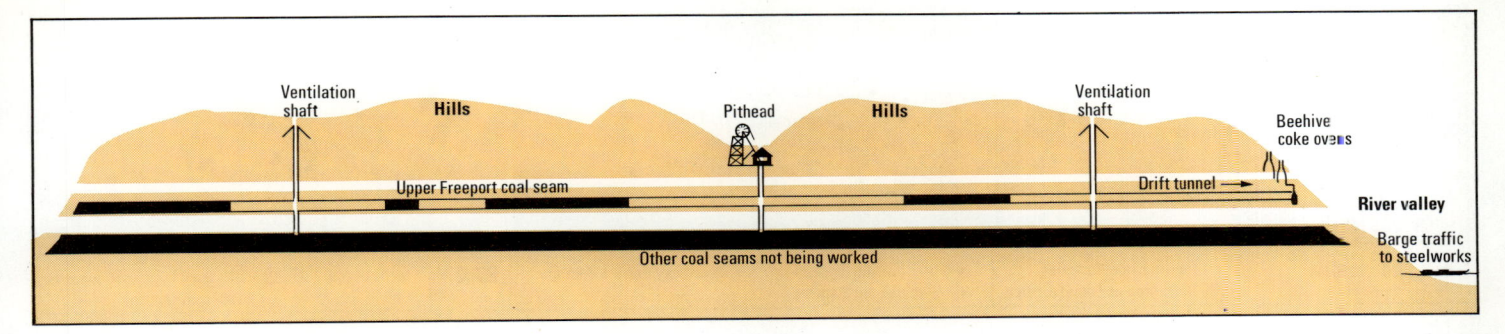

Fig. 34 The Upper Freeport coal seam in the Lucerne mine

of the miners live. Others live in the city of Indiana. The two hundred underground workers go down the Beck shaft to reach the coal seam. The other shafts are mainly for ventilation. The coal, however, is not taken out through the vertical shafts. In this area of Pennsylvania the coal seams lie flat and crop out on the valley sides so that horizontal tunnels, called drifts (Fig. 34), may be cut into the hillsides and the mined coal is carried out by means of small electric trains. The drift entrances are marked on the map.

In mining the coal, the 'room and pillar' method is used. The Upper Freeport seam is about 170 cm thick, with a 25 cm thick layer of shale in the middle. Only the coal below this shale layer is mined. Pillars and walls of coal are left in place to help support the roof of the mine. This coal can never be extracted. All the work of digging is done by machinery. The seam is bored with circular cutters and wheels, and the cut coal, as it falls, is taken from the cutting machine by an electric shuttle car and loaded onto endless conveyor belts which take the coal to the underground trains. The mine has 440 rail wagons and about 30 km of track underground. The mine works in three shifts each day, from 8 a.m. to 4 p.m., from 4 to 12 p.m., and from 12 midnight to 8 a.m. Not all the underground workers operate the coal diggers or trains. Many are needed to make the roof safe by jacking it up and supporting it with stout timber props and beams, or roof bolts. Ventilation is very important because the coal seam contains pockets of gas which would cause explosions if not cleared. Large exhaust fans are used in the air shafts to keep fresh air flowing to the mining areas. To keep dust down, the coalface being worked is sprayed constantly with water.

After being mined, the coal has to be cleaned, since a great deal of loose rock and dirt is mixed with it after digging. It is also screened, that is, sorted into various sizes. All this work is done mechanically.

Only about one third of the coal goes to make coke. The rest is used in power stations and to drive steam engines in factories. Coke is made in 'beehive' shaped ovens. There are 264 of these ovens operated by the Lucerne Coke Company, close to the mine (see map, Fig. 33).

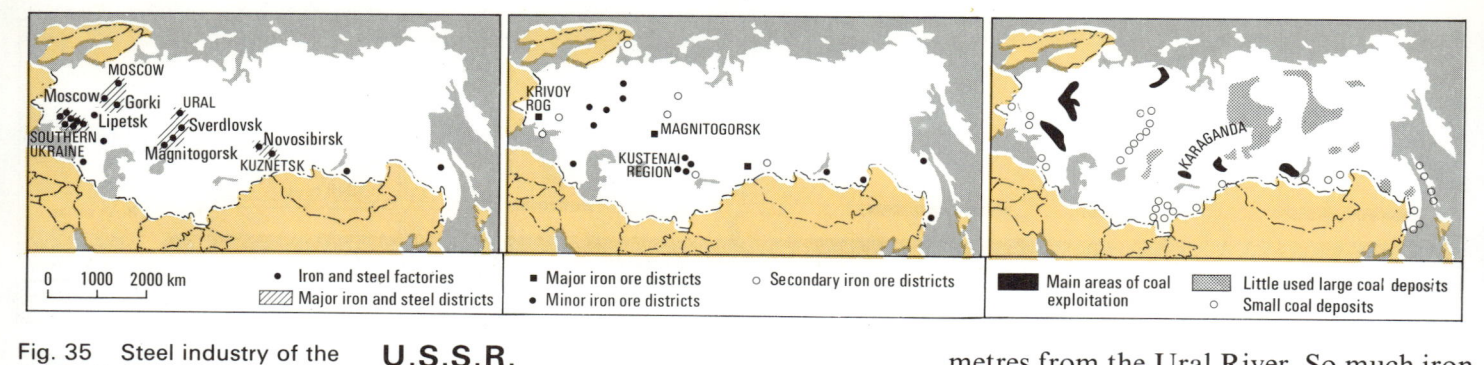

Fig. 35 Steel industry of the Soviet Union

Fig. 36 Steel output in the U.S.S.R.

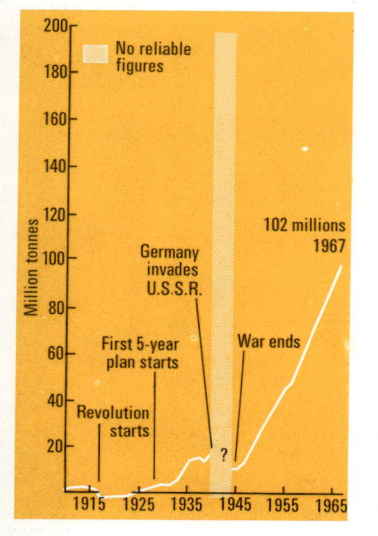

U.S.S.R.

In the U.S.S.R. the steel industry is more widely scattered than in the U.S.A. The chief centres are in the Donbass region and in the Ural Mountains. The Donbass is supplied with iron from Krivoy Rog and coal from the nearby very large coalfield. Coking coal from the Donbass is also taken by rail to the steel plants at Lipetsk, Moscow, and Gorki. Coal mining in the Donbass is not so easy as in Pennsylvania mines like the Lucerne. Although the Donbass seams are flattish and thick, they are deeper below ground and the coal has to be carried up vertical shafts rather than being rolled out horizontally. The Soviet mines are also less mechanized and require more human labour.

Magnitogorsk

In the Urals, the large city of Magnitogorsk is the main steel-producing centre; its blast furnaces were opened in 1932 as part of a five year plan (see p. 21). The map, Fig. 37, shows the layout of the works on the south side of the city. An important reason for building the steelworks here was the huge deposit of iron ore in the 'magnet mountain' a few kilometres from the Ural River. So much iron was present that compasses were affected by it and the city now takes its name from this feature. Huge open pits more than 2 km across have been excavated into the mountain, and most of the ore has now been taken. The steel mills are kept going by new iron mines in the Kustenai region (see Fig. 35) and large quantities of scrap steel are also fed into the furnaces along with the new iron.

All told, nearly 28 000 workers are employed at the Magnitogorsk steel plant. About 1100 of these, some of them women, work in the big open iron pits in the magnet mountain. The ore is excavated by electric digging machines, and these load it directly onto rail trucks. These are pulled to the ore **sintering plant** by electric locomotives. In the sintering plant the ore is first cleaned and separated from rock and dirt, then it is roasted with coke and limestone to begin the reduction process and drive off various impurities in the form of gas. The sintered ore, while still hot, is railed immediately to the eight blast furnaces, on the north side of the works. Conveniently placed between the coal yard where the trains from

Fig. 37

(a) Location of Magnitogorsk in the Ural Mountains

(b) The steel-producing city of Magnitogorsk

Kuznetsk and Karaganda arrive, and the blast furnaces, are 666 coke ovens. From these furnaces, where about 750 men work, the hot iron goes straight into the open hearth furnaces, along with scrap steel. Each furnace is managed by a team of men under a foreman, working on a three-shift system. In the open hearth furnaces, fiercely-burning jets of gas (the gas coming from the coke ovens and blast furnaces) re-melt the pig iron and scrap, the steel is purified and any necessary alloying metals are added. The molten steel is then poured out to be cast into huge blocks called **ingots**. These ingots, while still hot, are taken to a soaking pit, where they are 'soaked' with heat. If this was not done, each ingot would be at various temperatures; too cold on the outside, too hot inside, for rolling. When the ingot is at a suitable even heat right through, it is taken to the rolling mills where first it is rolled into a large slab or 'bloom'. The slab is then, after further re-heating if necessary, taken to other rolling mills where it may be rolled into plates, sheets, strips, rails, girders, and rods. The very thin sheet for making cans is rolled in the tin mill and electrically plated with tin there. Special steels are produced as required, liquid steel may be cast to make such items as locomotive wheels, and engine crankcases. Ingots may be forged (hammered into shape) by powerful steam-driven hammers to make shafts for marine engines, blades for turbines, and axles, and other solid metal machine parts.

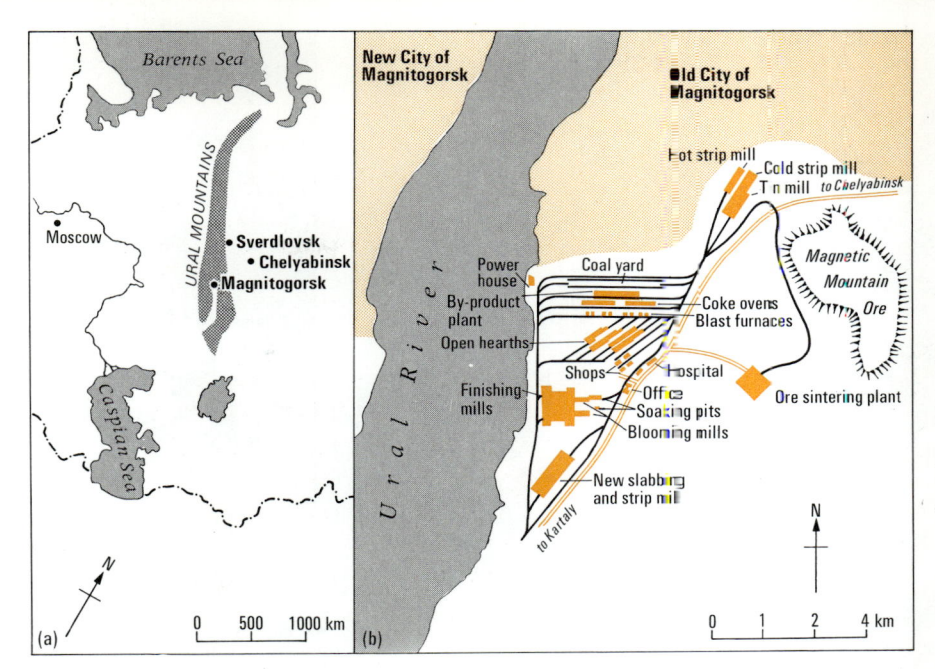

All this work is done at Magnitogorsk, but the steel is always sent on for further work to other cities, such as Chelyabinsk and Sverdlovsk. The castings and forgings invariably leave the works in a rough state. They need to be machined and drilled before being fitted into whatever piece of machinery or construction they are meant for. In the same way, Magnitogorsk makes tin plate, but not tins; the plated sheet metal is transported to the canning factory.

Photo. 123 Charging steel-making furnaces with molten iron in Cherepovets, 400 km north of Moscow

Fig. 38 The oil industry in the U.S.A., U.S.S.R. and China

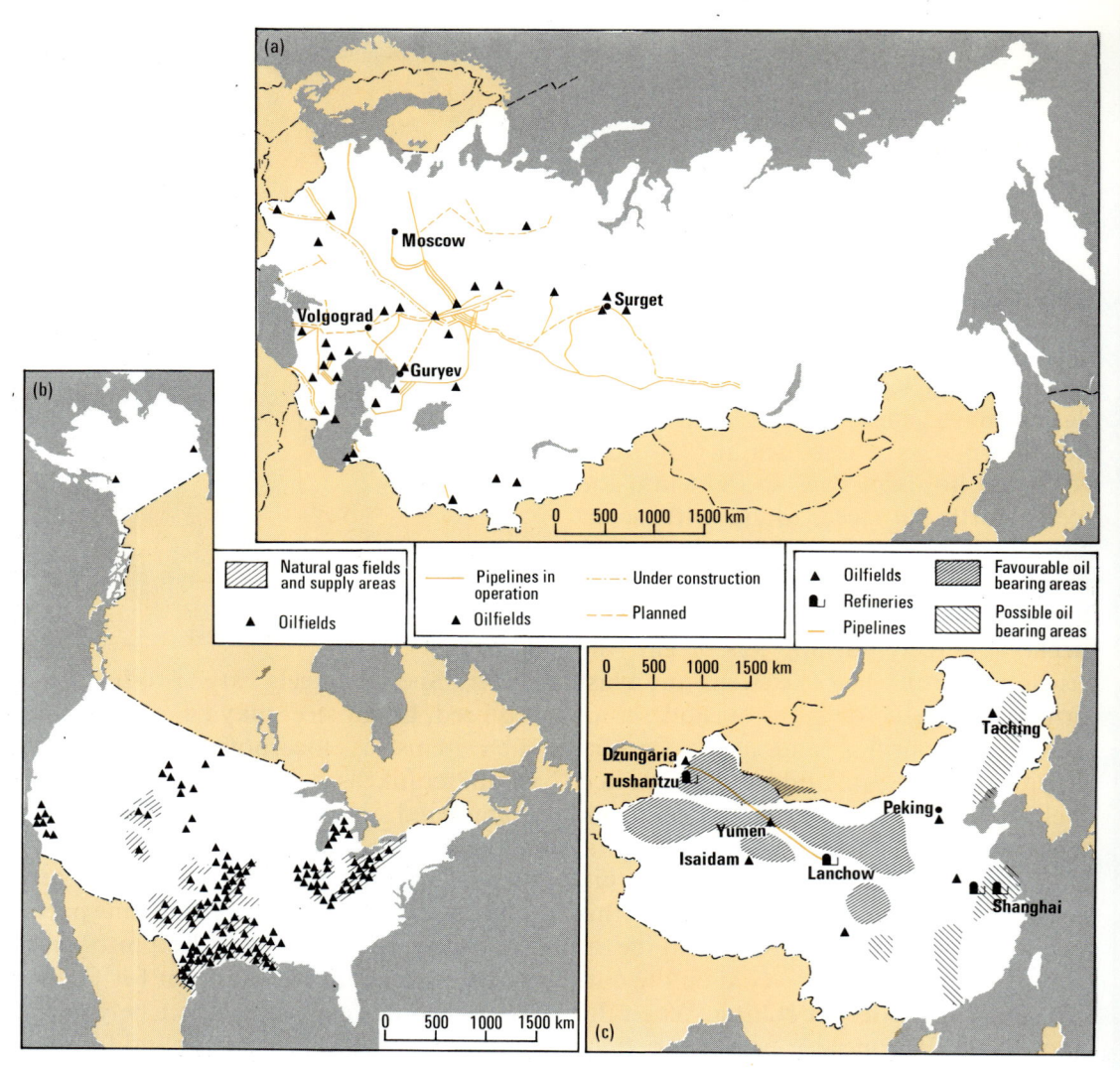

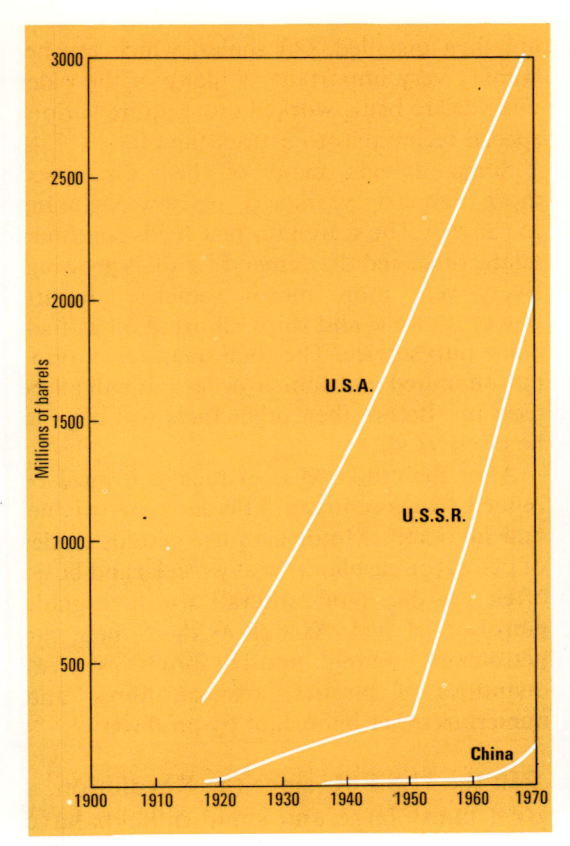

Oil

The first important oil find in the U.S.A. (and in the world) was in north-west Pennsylvania where a Mr. Drake opened his well in 1859. At this time there were no automobiles and the oil was used for such products as lubricants and leather dressing. Later, in the 1890s—by which time engines using petrol as fuel were becoming more common—new, very large fields were discovered in Texas, and in 1930 the oilfield which was to become the largest in the world was opened in east Texas. Thousands of wells were drilled every year so that by 1939 there were more than 26 000 of them. On average a new well goes on producing oil for about 27 years, and new ones are drilled in the U.S.A. at the rate of about 16 000 per year. The east Texas field is still one of the greatest oil-producing areas in the world, but the use of oil in the U.S.A. is so vast that huge quantities have to be imported from overseas, especially from Venezuela, Canada, and the Middle East. New discoveries in Alaska are likely to become very important, in spite of the great difficulties of working in such cold climates.

Photo. 124 This picture was taken in 1865 in Pennsylvania, not far from where the first major oil strike was made

Fig. 39 (left) Comparison of oil production in U.S.A., U.S.S.R. and China

The Oil Industry

Crude oil is found underground, trapped, often with natural gas and water, in porous rock layers and domes, or it may occur in oil shales, which are rocks of clay type impregnated with oil. The oil itself is a very complex liquid, varying in composition from place to place. Scientists believe it was formed from the decaying bodies of small creatures and plants which lived in the ancient seas and oceans where, many millions of years ago, these rocks were formed. To find oil-bearing rocks, geologists and geophysicists carry out extensive and difficult surveys. When they locate a possible oilfield they often do not know whether oil will actually be there. To make sure, exploratory wells are drilled. Sometimes gas, rather than oil, is found. If oil is present, it may rise to the surface under pressure, but as the liquid is taken out of the underground reservoir, and as more wells are drilled, the pressure may fall off and pumps are then installed. Oil shales, which are becoming very important as many of the older oilfields are being worked out, require various special techniques to extract the oil.

Some oilfields, many of them discovered more than sixty years ago, are now beginning to run dry. The search for new fields continues all the time, and the demand for oil is growing. Every year more motor vehicles, aircraft, power stations, and ships all using oil as fuel, come into service. The total quantity of oil is not unlimited and sooner or later it will all be used up. Before then other fuels will have to be discovered.

After the crude oil is extracted, it must be refined to make many different types of fuel and lubricant. Motor cars use certain grades of petrol (or gasoline); heavy trucks and buses often use diesel oil; aircraft use high-grade petrol or jet fuel. As well as these fuels, the petroleum refining industry produces great quantities of plastics, artificial fibres, and numerous other important by-products.

Photo. 125 Engineers at the remote control panel of the Novobakinsk oil refinery in Azerbaijan

In the U.S.S.R. since the Revolution, a great many large and small oilfields have been discovered and brought into production. The chief cities and centres of population, where most of the oil is used, are far away from the fields. In both the U.S.A. and the U.S.S.R., a great system of pipelines has been constructed to carry the fuel over long distances. (Similar, but separate, pipelines are built to distribute natural gas also.) In China, the oil industry is not yet greatly developed, but even so a similar problem exists. The largest fields are far away to the north-east around Taching in Manchuria, and to the far west at Karamai and Yumen in Sinkiang, and Kansu. A pipeline, nearly

Photo. 126 Oil workers drilling a well in south-western Latvia, U.S.S.R.

Photo. 127 (right, above) An American barge drills for offshore oil in Cook Inlet on the southern coast of Alaska. Oil has overtaken gold as Alaska's most important mineral

Photo. 128 (right below) Novobakinsk oil refinery in Azerbaijan

2000 km long, has been built through the deserts to reach Lanchow, where one of China's largest oil refineries is situated.

The maps (Fig. 38) show where the major oilfields lie, in all three giant nations. The graph (Fig. 39) shows how output compares and how it is increasing everywhere.

Fig. 40 The vehicle industry in the U.S.A.

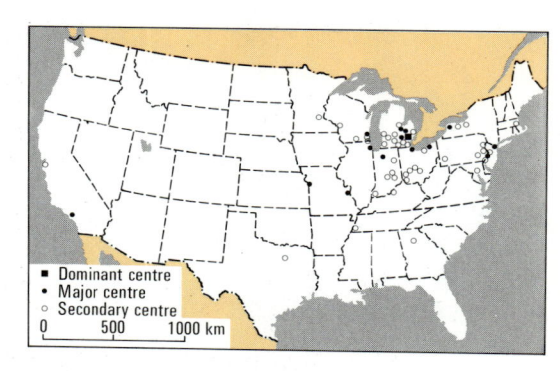

The Vehicle Industry

In the U.S.A., one of the most important industries, employing many thousands of workers and involving every part of the country to some extent, is the vehicle building industry. Most American families have at least one car; many have two or more. In addition the nation's transport system depends greatly on vans, heavy diesel-engined trucks and trailers, and long-distance buses. Some vehicle building companies have become so large and successful that they are known all over the world; Ford, General Motors, Chrysler have all established large works in other countries as well as the parent companies in the U.S.A.

In addition to the factories actually

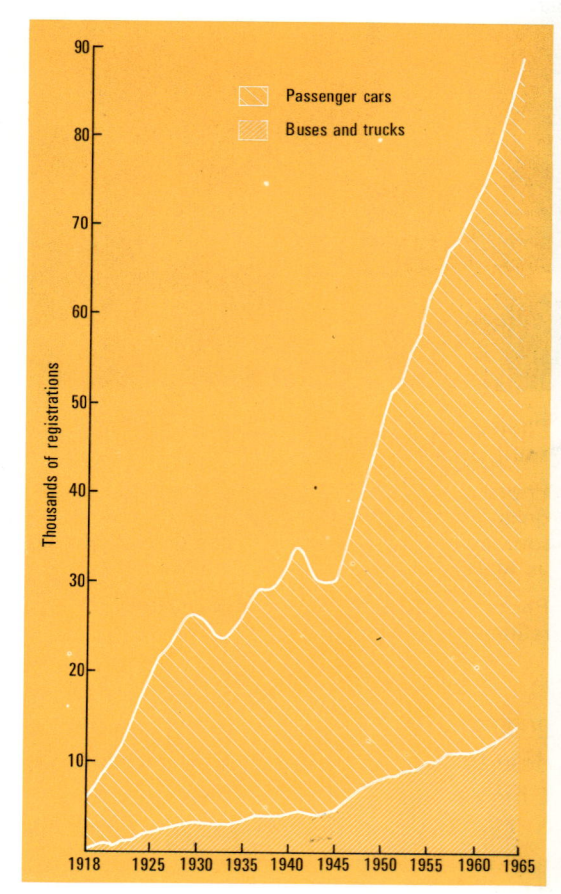

Fig. 41 Vehicle industry in the U.S.A.

building the vehicles, these companies have many thousands of showrooms in towns and cities, where their latest models can be displayed and sold. They employ great teams of salesmen, and operate (usually through agents) repair and service depots. The vehicle building industry is centred mainly on the city of Detroit, which was the place where Henry Ford set up his first mass-production factory. Steel for the industry is made in Detroit itself, the coal coming from Pennsylvania and the iron ore from Labrador and the Duluth region. To make one car, however, hundreds of other factories are needed as well as the main plant where the parts are assembled. As the map shows (Fig. 40), there are many other large centres building vehicles in the north-east of the U.S.A., and a few on the east and west coasts. There are many smaller centres, some specializing in body building, others making certain parts for engines, some making rubber tyres, and some glass.

Photo. 129 Mass-production of motor vehicles, Detroit, U.S.A.

Photo. 130 The assembly line in a Moscow motor works

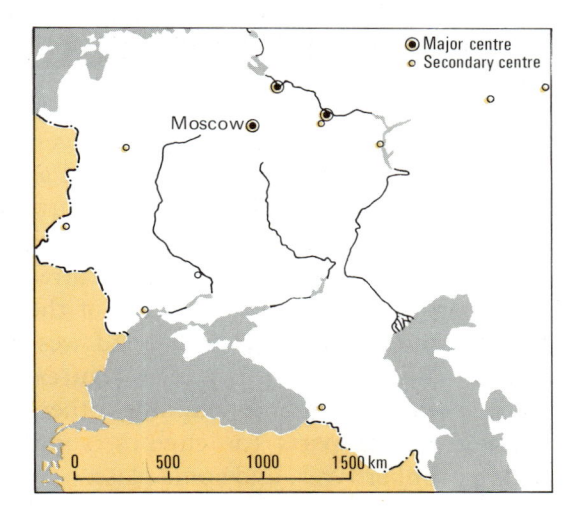

Fig. 42 The vehicle industry in the Soviet Union

In the U.S.S.R. the vehicle building industry is centred in Gorki and in Moscow. There are other important centres, but the plants in these two cities build more than half of all the vehicles in the U.S.S.R. The plant at Gorki is one of the largest in the world. Most of its output is trucks and buses rather than cars, which are chiefly made in Moscow. Mainly because the industry is controlled and owned by the state, the minor industries associated with vehicle building in the U.S.S.R. are usually part of the main factory, rather than being scattered over a wide area.

In China the motor vehicle is still rather an unusual sight over most of the country, though traffic is increasing in and near the big cities. Cars are quite rare, being restricted mainly to officials. A car does not usually belong to the man who uses it, but to his commune or to the central government. Trucks, buses, and tractors are considered far more important and there are large factories building these in Peking, Shanghai, and Changchun (about 300 km north-east of Shenyang in north-east China). The Chinese government believe that it is far more important to improve the farming methods in the country regions than to make motor cars. The vehicle factories therefore concentrate on building tractors. Some of these are similar to tractors in the U.S.A. or U.S.S.R., but such large machines are expensive and difficult to manage, and often they are only useful if there is another large machine, such as a harvester or heavy plough, to attach behind. Most communes in China are not rich enough to afford such equipment, and in many regions the fields are small, and sloping or terraced. To work in these conditions, it is better to have a small 'hand' tractor. These are cheap, easy to run and repair, and are much more suitable for Chinese farms. Some large tractors are built, however, for those communes which have large fields to work.

Photo. 131   Mass-produced hand-tractors in a Kiangsu factory. These tractors are suitable for gardens, orchards, and terraced fields

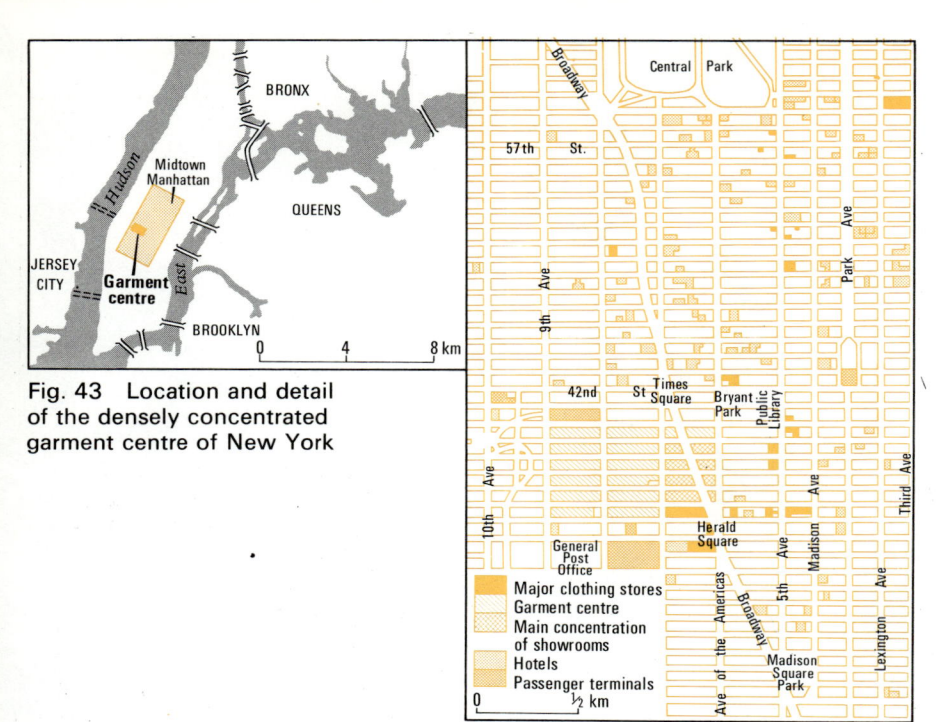

Fig. 43 Location and detail of the densely concentrated garment centre of New York

Light Industries

There are many different forms of light industry. It is impossible to describe them all. One such industry is the textile and clothing industry. Although most of the fibres used in making cloth come from cotton or sheep farms and from the oil industry (synthetic fibres), the actual spinning and weaving is usually done in the large cities. Peking is an important centre of cotton cloth manufacture.

The No. 2 Cotton Mill in Peking is one example of how the Chinese industry is organized. The mill employs 5300 people, nearly three-quarters of them women, mostly married. The mill has clinics and health centres for the workers, and there are kindergartens attached where the women can leave their young children while they work. The factory also has its own primary school, and altogether about 2400 children attend the factory schools and nursery.

The mill works six days a week, for $7\frac{1}{2}$ hours each day. There are 100 000 spindles for spinning cotton thread, and 2400 automatic looms. About 170 000 metres of cloth is produced each day.

The wages paid to workers in such a factory are low, but meals are provided in the canteen very cheaply, and rents for accommodation are also low.

Cloth from weaving mills is usually made up into garments in separate factories and small workshops. In New York, a small group of streets in mid-Manhattan (Fig. 43) contains hundreds of small clothing workshops and factories, very close to the large clothing and fashion shops on Broadway and 5th Avenue. This small district concentrates almost entirely on making clothing for women and children. It is said to be the most crowded industrial area in the world. More than 150 000 people are employed altogether, most of them in small factories with less

Item	Price U.S. $	Working time in days in China	Item	Price U.S. $	Working time in days in China
Man's shoes	10.00	$13\frac{3}{4}$	Child's romper suit	1.60	$2\frac{1}{4}$
Woman's walking shoes	9.60	13	Man's cap	1.80	$2\frac{1}{2}$
Woman's sandals	7.40	10	Man's cotton T-shirt	.80	1
Man's heavy overcoat	110.00	150	Child's cotton dress	1.00	$1\frac{1}{3}$
Woman's woollen overcoat	80.00	109	Cotton socks	.50	$\frac{1}{2}$
Man's shirt	4.00	$5\frac{1}{2}$	Hand cart	50.00	60
Man's pyjamas	5.00	$6\frac{3}{4}$	Bicycle	71.00	93
Man's suit	56.00	$76\frac{3}{4}$	Woman's trouser suit	42.00	$57\frac{1}{2}$
Man's topcoat	43.50	$59\frac{1}{2}$	Woollen socks	2.20	3

Table 5 Comparative costs of some everyday items in America and China. Find out the exchange rate for dollars and pounds; this changes from time to time

than 20 other people. Some of the back-street workshops concentrate on producing buttons or zip fasteners; others will buy these to use in garments which are tailored and sewn, mainly by women workers, with electric machines. As fashion in women's clothing changes, the small firms find it very difficult to keep going; a factory owner who has bought, from the cloth industry, a large amount of a certain fabric, may find it left on his hands if the fashion changes. His small company may go bankrupt. Another who guesses correctly what sort of clothing will be popular, may make a fortune. The workers in the industry thus find things changing from day to day, not only in the style of costumes they are making, but often in the company they work for—if one employer goes bankrupt, his firm will probably be taken over by another.

In the U.S.S.R. while the textile spinning and weaving mills are very widely scattered, the large cities, especially Moscow, have the leading clothing manufacturing workshops. With a socialist system, changes in fashion are neither so frequent nor so rapid as in the U.S.A., and the clothing industry thus tends to be much more stable.

Assignments

1. Compare the kinds of work done in different industries as shown in the photographs in this chapter.

2. Find out what industries there are near your own home and school. What kind of work is done by people in these industries?

3. Study the list of items shown in the table above (Table 5), and compare the figures with those which apply to your own family. Suppose that a Chinese worker has to work for 93 days to buy himself a bicycle. Then find out how much a cheap bicycle costs in your local shops, and work out how many days' work an ordinary working man would have to do to earn this sum (e.g., if a bicycle costs £30, a man earning £5 would need to work for 6 days to earn this. Of course, he would need money for other things too during this period; the method is only intended as a rough guide for comparison of living costs).

Fig. 44 (a) Railways of the U.S.S.R. Note how the lines radiate from Moscow. Why are there so few railways in the east, north, and south?
(b) the forty largest cities of the U.S.S.R. Thirty nine are shown here with Khabarovsk, far to the east, shown in 44(a)

Fig. 45 (a) Railways of the U.S.A. (b) the major cities of the U.S.A.

Fig. 46 (a) Compared with the U.S.A. and U.S.S.R., China has few railways. Peking is well-placed between the heavy industrial areas of Manchuria, and the rest of the country. Why are there so few railways in the west? The Yangtse Kiang is shown as a navigable waterway. Why is this important to Shanghai? (b) The major cities of China

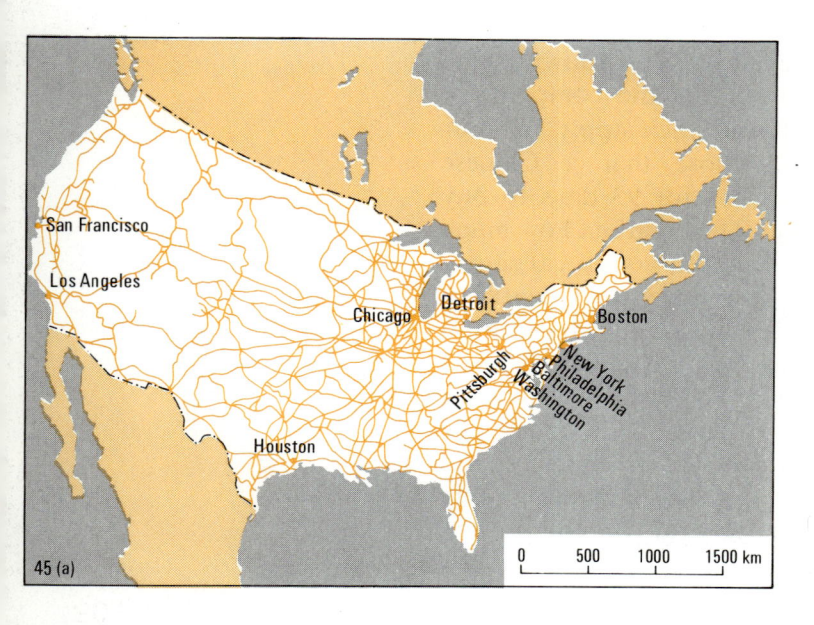

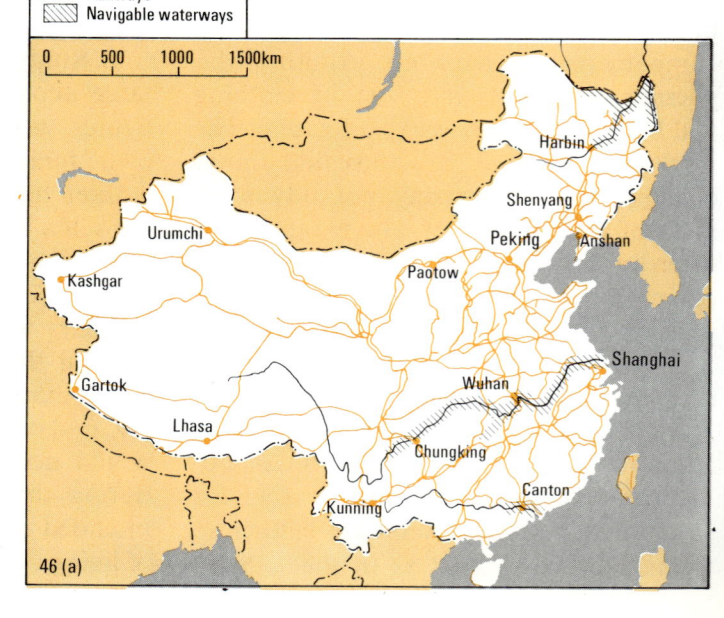

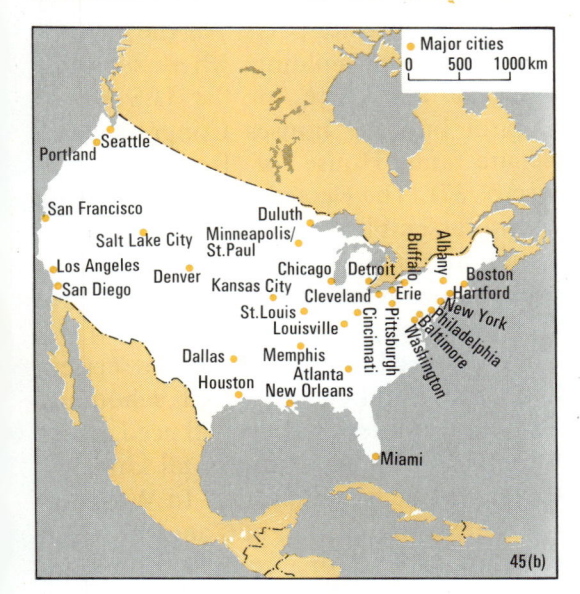

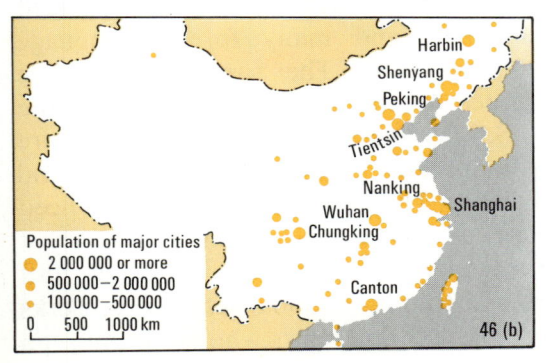

8 Growing Cities

In some ways, all modern cities are alike; they are great concentrations of people and buildings with many shops, offices, houses and flats, hospitals, schools, colleges and other public buildings, with crowded streets and heavy traffic. The thing that brings the city people together is usually the kind of work the city as a whole does. Some cities have only one or two main **functions**; the city of Magnitogorsk (see p. 98) is mainly a steel-making city. There are many people in Magnitogorsk who do not work in the steel plant or the iron quarries, for this city, like any other, has shops, schools, and bus services. The steel plant, however, is the main reason for the city to be where it is. Some other cities, especially very large ones, have many different functions. For example, London is the capital city of Britain; it is also a port, and an important centre of industry and banking, a centre of entertainment, of art galleries and museums.

Photo. 132 Modern 26-storey office blocks and flats in Moscow.

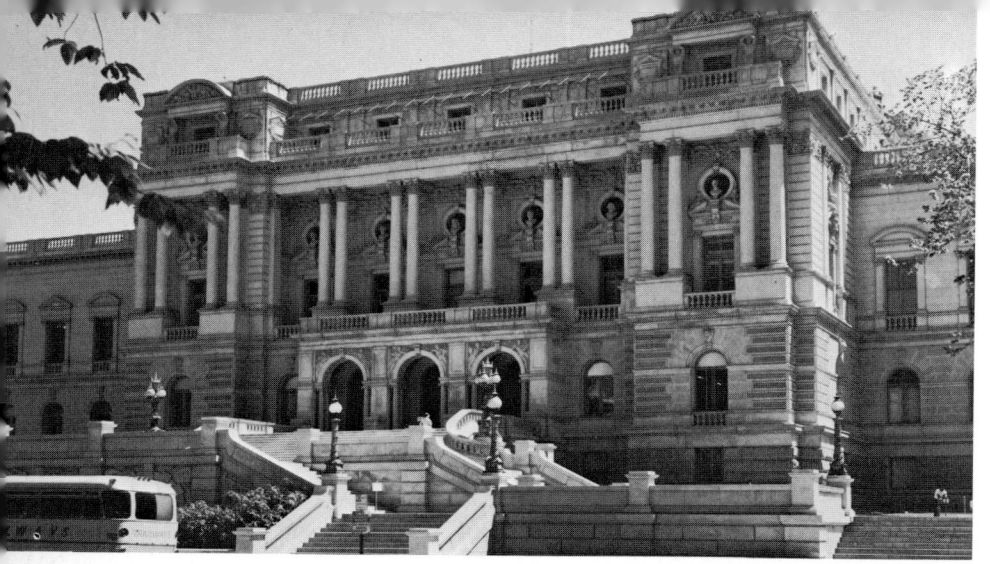

Photo. 133. The Library of Congress in Washington

Photo. 134 Old and new buildings, side by side in Eastern Peking. Even the main streets have little traffic other than electric trolley buses and trucks

The capitals

Peking, **Washington** and **Moscow** are capital cities. They have other important functions, but since they are all capitals, they have certain features in common. As these cities fulfil similar purposes, they use the same kinds of buildings, even though they may differ in other ways, because of history, language, and situation.

All governments need to meet in some central place where they can discuss and decide matters affecting the whole country and all its separate parts. All the capitals thus have large buildings where such discussions take place; in the U.S.A. the Capitol building houses Congress, both Senate and House of Representatives (see p. 37). The elected members of these central assemblies come from all over the nation and may not regard the capital as their home. Nevertheless, they will have to spend a large part of their time there. They will need housing and other services and their children will need schooling. These government officers will need access to books and information of all kinds, so there must be large libraries. In Washington there is the Library of Congress which contains at least one copy of every important book published in the English language, and many foreign language volumes also. The same services are needed for the national assemblies in the U.S.S.R. and China, and so there are government libraries in Moscow and Peking. The government libraries need large staffs, and each senior member of the government, or minister, needs staff to assist him—personal secretaries, clerks and typists, assistants who advise him on special problems, and often scientists and scholars who are particularly expert in some area. Thus, around the government itself there grows up a very important group of advisory staff who work for the government and help it to make its decisions. These people are not, as a rule, elected by the people but are employed as **civil servants**.

A minister may have several hundred people in his advisory department, and many more to administer the laws. If, for example, there is a change in the taxation laws, arrangements must be made to collect the taxes, check that instructions are sent to every part of the nation and, of course, to make sure that the money does come in. The government as a whole needs many thousands of people for this kind of work, and the capital city must have offices for them to work in and must provide housing, schools, hospitals, and all other services for them.

A modern capital city must also provide for **foreign embassies**. Countries, whether friendly or not, need to keep in touch with one another, and most countries send an ambassador to the capital cities of other major nations.

The capital is also usually the headquarters, in peacetime, of the **armed services**. The huge Pentagon building in Washington is the most obvious example of this. The national **police forces** and **security services** will also have offices in the capital, and since so many government decisions affect industry and agriculture, the capital city often houses offices of all the main **business concerns**, **trade unions** and other national bodies, such as banks and insurance companies. In a communist state, many of these are in fact government departments themselves, but this does not greatly alter the kind of work that has to be done, nor the kind of buildings needed to house the staff.

Photo. 35 Washington, D.C., capital city of the United States. Note the Capitol building with its dome, and the numerous other large government offices. Washington is the centre of government, but unlike the other capitals, not of the arts or business. These interests are centred in New York, the commercial heart of the nation.

113

Photo. 136   The Washington Monument

Photo. 137   St. Basil's Cathedral in Moscow's Red Square, with Lenin's tomb in the foreground, and the Kremlin on the right. Note the modern buildings in the background

Modern government depends on **communication**. Elected representatives and government officials must be able to travel easily from their offices to all the parts of the country they control, and often overseas as well. The capital needs one or more large airports capable of handling all sorts of traffic, and it is also a major centre of telephone and telegraph systems, and of radio and television broadcasting. Major newspapers and magazines, covering the whole country, are likely to be based in the capital, especially in the communist countries where communications **media** are under direct control of the government. In addition, the government needs to print and publish its own papers, pamphlets, instructions, and books, so any capital city of a large nation has an important printing and publishing industry.

It is natural for the people of the nation to look towards the capital as a centre in other ways as well. **National monuments** and museums, for instance, are often sited in the capital: in Moscow, Lenin's tomb is visited by many thousands of people every year; in Washington there are the Washington Monument and the Lincoln Memorial; Peking has the Sun Yat Sen Park, a memorial to the leader of the first Chinese revolution of 1911, and the Great Hall of the People nearby. Apart from monuments, a capital city is often the national centre for the arts and entertainment. This is especially true of Moscow, which has world famous theatre and ballet companies, and concert orchestras. China, too, has national theatre and dance companies based in Peking, but in the U.S.A. the city of New York, rather than Washington, is recognized as the centre of the theatrical arts.

Photo. 138 The Guggenheim Museum of modern art on Fifth Avenue, New York. Visitors take a lift to the top, and walk round the gently-descending spiral gallery to the ground

Photo. 139 Revolutionary ballet in China. Note the stage backdrop with its picture of Mao Tse-tung

Fig. 47 The central area of Peking

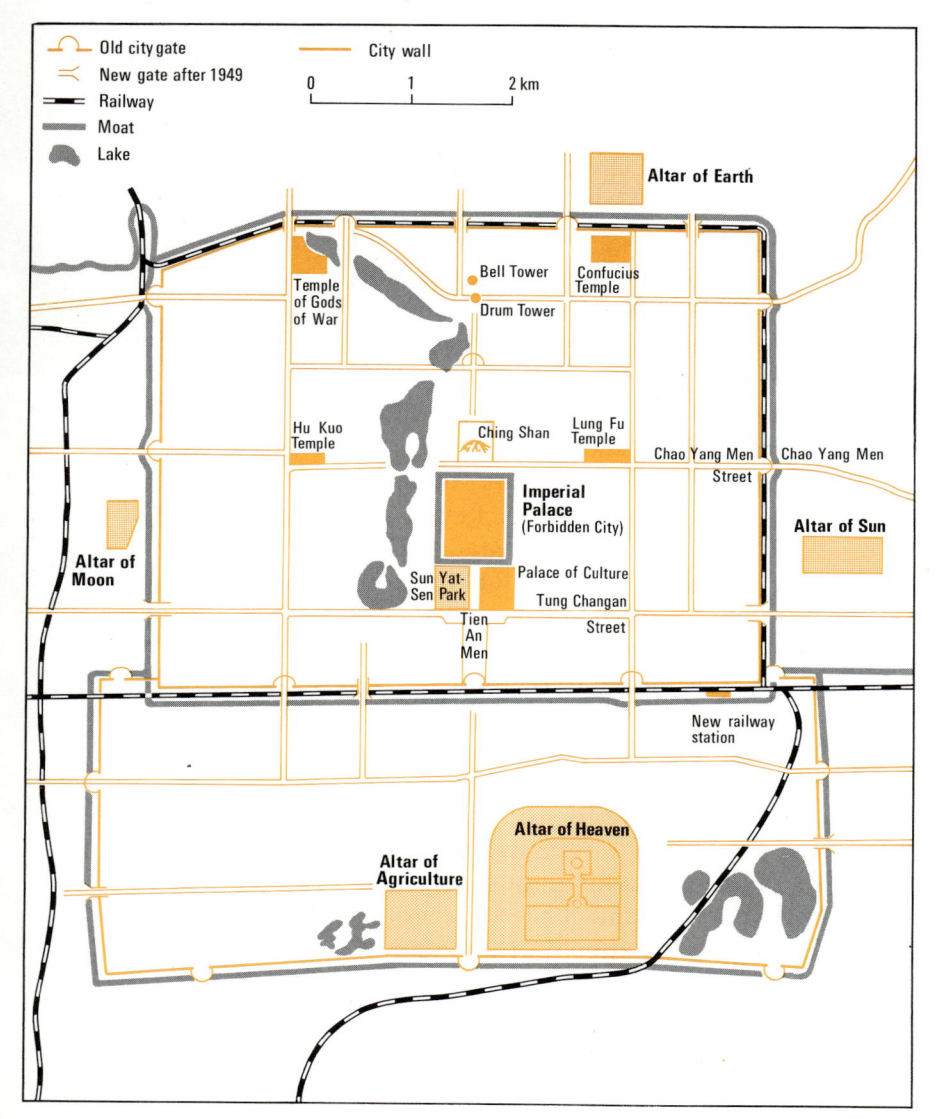

The three capitals thus resemble each other in many ways. Both Peking and Moscow are ancient cities which, for a variety of reasons, were chosen by the communist governments to be capitals of the new state. The old city walls can still be seen in Peking, and the modern road pattern of Moscow has circular ring roads which follow the line of the walls that once stood around the city. The government of both these nations is carried on today very largely from inside the old centres; in Moscow the old fortress of the Kremlin, surrounded by its high brick walls; in Peking the 'forbidden city', which, in the time of the Chinese emperors, was forbidden to all Europeans. Washington, on the other hand, was a city built from the first as a capital, after the War of Independence. The first large buildings to appear were the White House, where the presidents of the U.S.A. have lived ever since, and the Capitol building. The city was laid out with broad avenues and streets, parks and formal gardens, and although it has grown far larger than the original planners expected, the layout of the central area remains and looks very different from either of the older capitals.

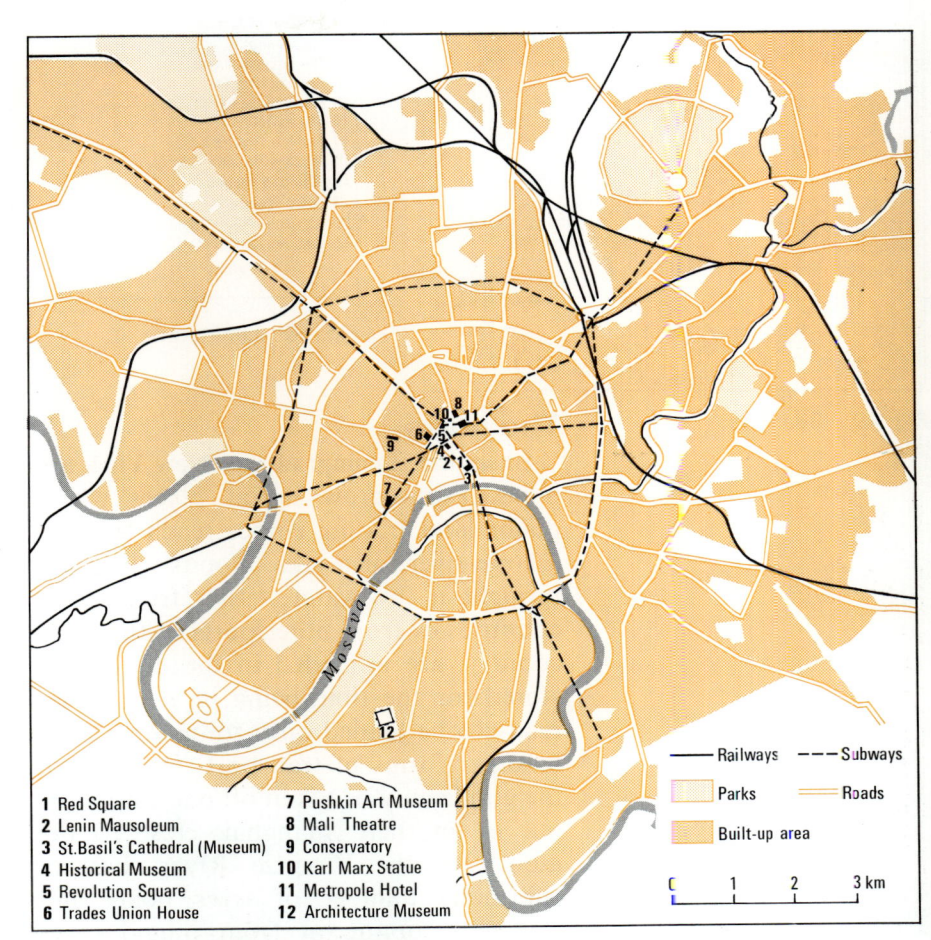

Fig. 48 The central area of Moscow

Fig. 49 Shanghai

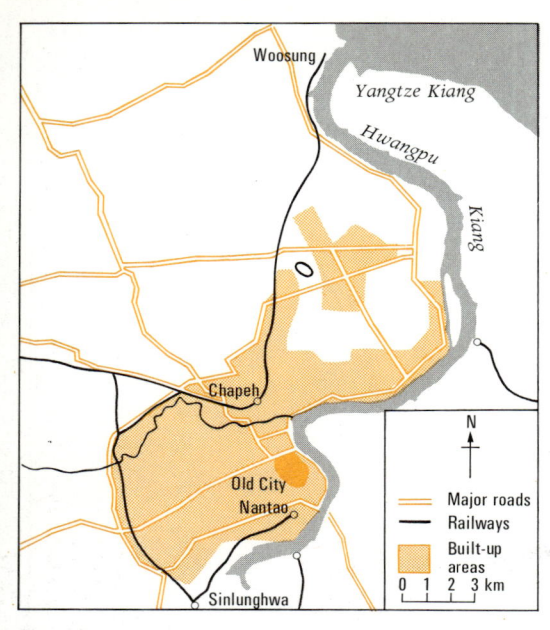

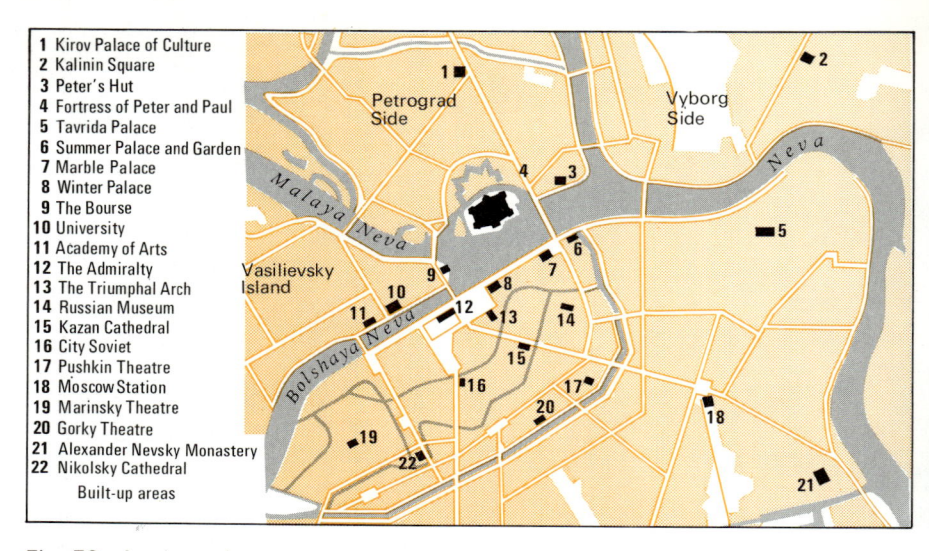

Leningrad map key:
1 Kirov Palace of Culture
2 Kalinin Square
3 Peter's Hut
4 Fortress of Peter and Paul
5 Tavrida Palace
6 Summer Palace and Garden
7 Marble Palace
8 Winter Palace
9 The Bourse
10 University
11 Academy of Arts
12 The Admiralty
13 The Triumphal Arch
14 Russian Museum
15 Kazan Cathedral
16 City Soviet
17 Pushkin Theatre
18 Moscow Station
19 Marinsky Theatre
20 Gorky Theatre
21 Alexander Nevsky Monastery
22 Nikolsky Cathedral
Built-up areas

Fig. 50 Leningrad

The ports

Shanghai, **Leningrad** and **New York** are ports. Ports grow up at places where major land trading routes reach the sea, a large river, or a lake. Goods which are brought in by water, either from other countries or from other ports of the same country, are unloaded in the docks and stored for the time being in warehouses ready to be loaded onto trains or trucks, or other forms of transport. Quite often the goods may be taken off one ship to be put in another. Shanghai, close to the mouth of the Yangtze River, has an enormous number of river boats and steamers coming in from inland cities such as Nanking, Wuhan, and Chungking, and the goods from these are often taken by coastal steamers and other vessels from the port along the coast to Canton, Tientsin, and other towns and cities.

A port must have a good harbour with water deep enough for various types of ship. The land near the harbour must be firm enough for cranes, warehouses, and other buildings to stand safely. Many potentially good harbours are spoiled because the coastline is swampy or liable to flood at high tide, or because rivers choke the channels with silt and mud. Equally important, the port must be connected in some way with its **hinterland**, the land area to and from which the goods and passengers move. In the case of Shanghai, the Yangtze Kiang is the main connection with the hinterland; New York depends mainly on roads and railways now, though a large canal to the Great Lakes was important for the earlier growth of the city; Leningrad has good road and rail links with Moscow itself.

Photo. 140 Shanghai dockers load produce for export

Photo. 141 Dockside workers in New York take a break between jobs

Photo. 142   In the shipyards of Leningrad

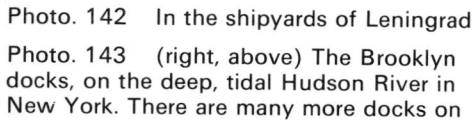

Photo. 143   (right, above) The Brooklyn docks, on the deep, tidal Hudson River in New York. There are many more docks on the New Jersey side of the river

Photo. 144   (right, below) The Shanghai waterfront

Photo. 145 The Treasury building and Wall Street, New York. Few people live in these office buildings, and at night the business centre is nearly deserted

Apart from the docks and the transport services, where goods are being moved from one sort of transport to another, it is often convenient to process them in some way. Shanghai has large grain mills where bulk wheat is ground into flour before being despatched to bakeries, there are cotton spinning and weaving mills where raw cotton is made into cloth, and oil refineries where crude oil is made into petrol and lubricants. In this way, ports tend to become **centres of industry**, and workers are needed for the factories as well as for the docks themselves. Ship and boat repairing, too, is a usual function of a port, but actual shipbuilding is usually sited close to large steelworks because it depends on the steel industry.

As **centres of trade**, large ports also become important centres of banking and finance. Most of the chief banks and insurance companies of the U.S.A. have their head offices in New York, especially in the Wall Street area, and the Stock Exchange is there also. While the political capital is in Washington, in many ways New York, which is a far larger city than the capital, is the centre of American business. In the communist countries all

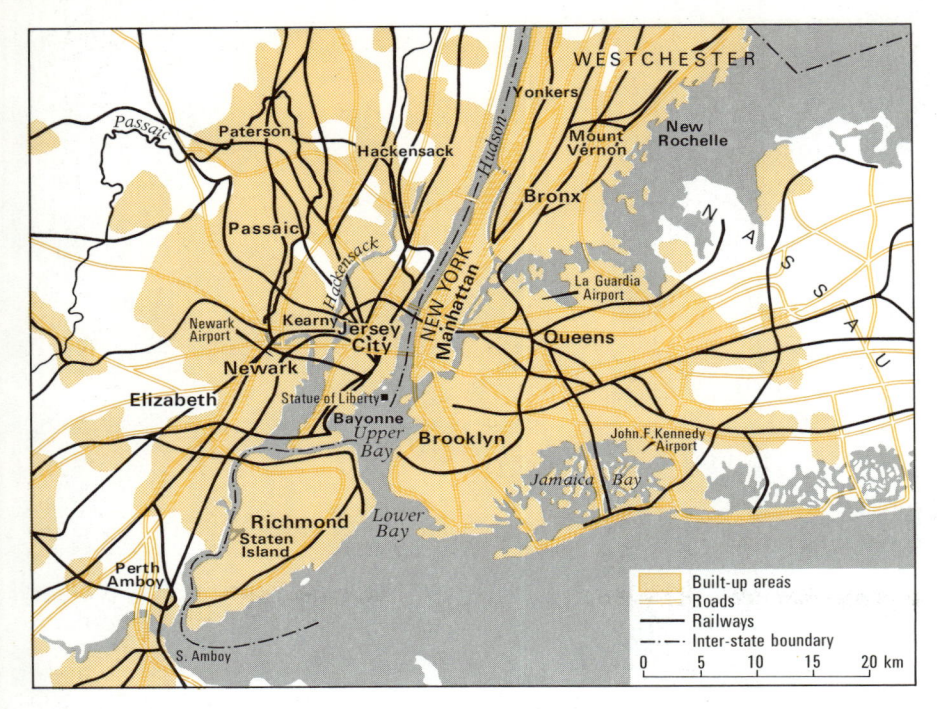

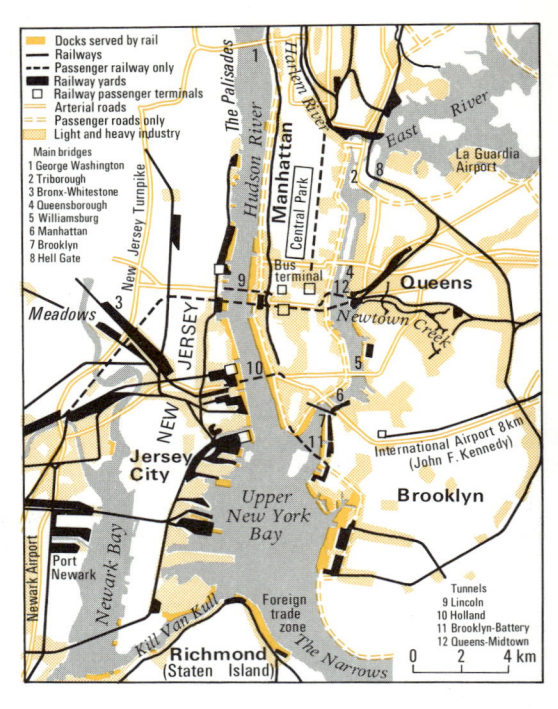

Fig. 51 (above) New York city and suburbs

Fig. 52a (above right) The dock areas of New York, and the main roads and railways that serve them

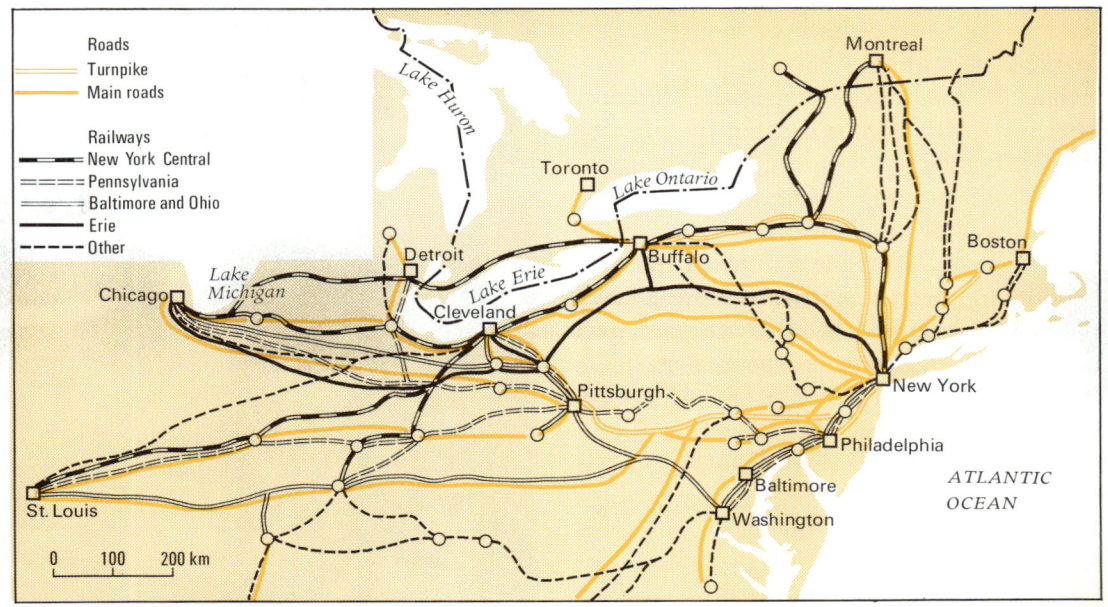

Fig. 52b (right) Roads and railways connect New York with numerous other cities

financial matters are under political control so there is no area like Wall Street, but Shanghai took advantage of being an important trading centre and developed manufacturing so that it has grown now to be the largest city in the world. Leningrad, however, is much smaller than Moscow. One reason for this is that the U.S.S.R. has less sea trade than either China or the U.S.A. Almost everything needed in the U.S.S.R. is either grown, manufactured, or mined within the frontiers. The land area of the Union is so large, extending from the deserts and mountains of the south to the Arctic, that nearly every important kind of crop can be harvested somewhere, except those requiring a tropical or semi-tropical climate. For example, rubber, cane sugar, and cacao are imports. Vital minerals are found in such quantities that there is no need for imports, but sea trade may be opened up because the U.S.A., Japan, and Western Europe are interested in buying the oil and natural gas found in Siberia.

The three ports, having similar functions, are alike in some ways, but the differences are very important also. Leningrad, under the Czars, was the Capital of Russia and the old palace remains as a museum. Like Washington, Leningrad, or St. Petersburg as it was before the Revolution, was a planned city, laid out in 1703, and the street plan of the present day shows this clearly, a great contrast with the irregular plan of Shanghai, which grew up round an old fishing village without any special planning. New York began on a small island (Manhattan) at the mouth of the Hudson River and the small space available encouraged the growth of skyscrapers. The city now has grown far beyond Manhattan Island and the docks are on both sides of the Hudson.

Photo. 146 Central Shanghai. Although China is no longer an important trading nation, so much industry was developed in Shanghai when trading was active, that it has grown to be the largest city in the world

Photo. 147 The dense industry of Pittsburgh. Pittsburgh is no longer the main centre of U.S. steel-making. Vast amounts are produced by the cities of the Great Lakes, especially Chicago. These are closer to local iron ore, and coal and iron can be shipped in easily. Therefore they are in a better position to serve the market—the buyers—of raw steel. Recent anti-pollution laws have reduced the smoke since this photograph was taken

Industrial cities

Maps in Chapter 7 show the positions of the main industrial regions of the three giant powers. Associated with all these are many important towns and cities. Such cities tend to take their character from the type of industry that goes on, so that in spite of political and climatic differences, they are sometimes more like one another than they are like the capital cities or ports in the same country. The people who work in an industrial city, wherever it is, live very differently from country and farm workers nearby, or from the government officials and public servants in the capitals. The jobs done in a city like **Shenyang**, **Sverdlovsk**, or **Pittsburgh** are often exactly the same.

Such cities are also alike in that they are centres of communications. The raw materials must be brought into the works. The products of the steel mills and factories must be moved away to all parts of the country, and sometimes overseas.

Pittsburgh, in the U.S.A., stands at the junction of three large rivers, the Allegheny, the Monongahela and the Youghiogheny, where they join to form the Ohio. Each river has carved itself a deep and broad valley through the surrounding uplands, providing easy routes for roads and railways as well as allowing barge traffic on the rivers themselves. Coal and coke for the steel furnaces comes from very large, mechanized mines in the uplands. Iron ore was found locally when

> Find the cities mentioned in this section, on maps earlier in the book, or in an atlas.

the city was new, but now most of it comes long distances from the mining city of Duluth or from the iron fields of Canada, via ships on the St. Lawrence Seaway and the Great Lakes, and thence by rail from the shores of Lake Erie. Raw steel from Pittsburgh goes along the valleys to cities such as Cincinnati, Albany and Buffalo, which have large engineering industries, and Pittsburgh itself has works making machine tools, motor-car parts, and other machinery. These products leave the city by road or rail for sale all over the U.S.A. The centre of Pittsburgh, a small area of land between the Allegheny and the Monongahela rivers where they join, is often called the Golden Triangle; it is one of the most expensive places to buy property in the U.S.A. The value of the triangle depends on the steelworks and machine shops of the industrial parts of the city.

Sverdlovsk, too, is a centre of railways in a highland region, the central Ural Mountains, and these uplands are the source of some of the raw materials, iron ore, copper, and some gold. Coal is less plentiful and a great deal has to come from the Kuznetsk area 1500 km to the east. Sverdlovsk has some steel mills, but the main work is engineering, using the raw steel brought in from the scattered steel-making towns of the regions to north and south. Unlike Pittsburgh, Sverdlovsk is away from the main centres of population of the country (see population map on p. 14), so its products have to be transported more than 1000 km westwards before reaching the areas where they are most needed. Sverdlovsk is in a region of long, cold winters. The city thus faces difficulties much more severe than those of Pittsburgh.

Photo. 148 New blocks of workers' flats under construction in Sverdlovsk

Photo. 149 Shenyang. A street scene in the city centre

Shenyang is in a cold upland region, 90 km north of the steel-making city of Anshan. Iron ore and coal for steel-making are found in the hills; railways from Anshan bring the steel to Shenyang, and the factories there are connected by rail to the rest of China, and to the port of Dairen. Shenyang, which was called Mukden before the Revolution, began very differently from Pittsburgh or Sverdlovsk. Before 1644 it was the capital of the Manchu emperors who set up the last Ch'ing dynasty. On the west side of the modern industrial city the old imperial palace still remains, with ancient government buildings which once were enclosed, like those in Peking and Moscow, by a high wall.

Shenyang, like Sverdlovsk, is far from the main population centres of the country it serves. Peking is about 800 km away, Shanghai more than twice as far.

Photo. 150   Lake Meadows housing estate in Chicago

Problems of growing cities

All the cities mentioned in this chapter are growing, some very rapidly. Washington has grown from about 1½ million people in 1960 to nearly 3 million in 1970; Shanghai was over 6 million in 1953 and is over 10 million now; Moscow has grown from under 6 million to well over 7 million people in 12 years. Such growth leads to many serious problems. Houses and flats must be built; if there are too few there will be overcrowding and bad health. Shortages of clean water and food arise, there is too much pressure on schools, shops, hospitals, and other services. In the streets there is too much traffic; the roads designed for a small town are required to serve a much bigger population; even pavements and side-

Photo. 151   Compare this photo of Shanghai with Photo. 150. As in Chicago the slums are being replaced by new flats. As soon as the modern building is finished, the old houses will be demolished

Photo. 152 An uncommon sight in New York. This poor Harlem black transports his possessions in a hand-cart. Note the lanes of traffic and the big cars in the background

Photo. 153 Cars parked in cities are responsible for much congestion. Strict time limits must be enforced by traffic wardens such as this woman in Chicago

walks can become too narrow to cope with the increased numbers of pedestrians. Widening the roads means knocking down buildings which can make the housing shortage worse. Even if the road system can be arranged to take the volume of traffic, fumes and dirt from the motors can become so thick that breathing is difficult. Because the U.S.A. is a rich country and almost everyone has a car, problems of this sort have developed there before appearing in either the U.S.S.R. or China, where there are fewer cars and less traffic. Nevertheless, there is very serious over-crowding in Shanghai and many other Chinese cities, and as the two communist powers develop and expand their industries still more, it seems likely that they, too, will encounter the same troubles as those of the capitalist world.

Photo. 154 Mobile homes on the Los Angeles River in California. This is one way of solving the problem of housing a rapidly growing population. But it is only a temporary measure, and great pressure is placed on local services such as schools and hospitals. Note the complex highway system

Photo. 155 Apartment blocks in the Ming Hong district of Shanghai. This is a 'satellite town', designed to house and employ some of the vast population of Shanghai

Photo. 156 Peking. Bicycles cause no pollution and take less space than cars, as well as being much cheaper

Pollution

In all three giant powers, the cities are growing. In this they are alike, but the U.S.A. seems to have reached a stage where the cities have grown too much. The centres of many American cities have been completely taken up by office blocks and highways; no one lives in the central business district; at night and at weekends the heart of such a city is dead. Yet each working day the streets are jammed as people rush to work from their homes in the suburbs. Fumes and noise from vehicles become almost unbearable. The huge American city will have to be changed and controlled. In the U.S.S.R. so far these problems have not become desperate. Even Moscow, which is the largest city, has not yet developed traffic problems as serious as those in smaller American cities; this is mainly because fewer Soviet families own motor cars and so they rely on public transport. However, more traffic appears each year, as the nation becomes more prosperous. It may be that the Soviet government will learn from American experience and will make long-term plans to limit the use of cars. In China the problem of the growing city is different, because many Chinese cities are already very large indeed. They have never depended on motor traffic, and very few Chinese people ever use cars. As the country becomes more industrialized, the government will have to decide whether huge cities like Shanghai, Peking, and Canton, can be reconstructed with major highways and facilities for the increased motor traffic, or whether somehow the car can be kept out of the city altogether, with a very efficient system of public transport developed instead. It seems, therefore, that each of the three powers, facing the problem of city growth, will work out its own solution.

Assignments

1. Discuss with your teacher the reasons why cities grow. Do the same reasons apply in both communist and capitalist countries? Could a really strong government force or persuade people to move away from the bigger cities to smaller towns? Would this be a good way to plan for the future?

2. From the photographs and plans in this chapter, make a list of the main buildings and features of the three capital cities illustrated which distinguish them from other types of cities. Where possible, give the actual name of the buildings in each of Washington, Moscow, and Peking.

3. Leningrad and Washington were both planned as capital cities. In what ways do they resemble each other? What reasons can you think of for choosing either as the capital of its country? From reference books, find out why they were chosen. Do the reasons given at the time of the choice still apply today?

4. What reasons can you discover for the choice, by the communists, of Moscow and Peking as capitals of the U.S.S.R. and China? Would Shanghai, as the biggest city, have been a better choice than Peking? Why did the government of the U.S.S.R. move the capital from St. Petersburg (Leningrad) to Moscow?

Photo. 157 Moscow's traffic problem is growing, but is not yet as serious as in the large American cities

9 Satellites and Allies

The three giant powers sometimes seem very much alike in their relationships with the rest of the world. Each one tries to surround itself with allies or even **satellites**. A satellite nation is one which is strongly controlled by one of the giant powers. Large parts of the globe are not committed to any one of the three giants, and in these regions they all try to increase their influence. One way in which this is done is by sending aid of various kinds. In Tanzania Chinese engineers helped to build a railway; in Egypt aid from the U.S.S.R., both in money and equipment, and in the form of expert designers and engineers, has helped to build the great Aswan Dam; the U.S.A. has given similar aid to many regions of India, Africa, Latin America, and the Middle East.

Military influence

Aid is usually given for some additional reason, or motive. Each of the giant powers hopes that by helping under-developed nations it will gain influence over them. This would increase the giant's power even further.

Sometimes the offer of help is accompanied by a military alliance, involving the siting of military units in the country concerned, or the attachment of military experts to the staff of the home forces. So the Soviet help at Aswan was accompanied by an agreement to supply arms and military advisers to the United Arab Republic, and in 1962 a very dangerous situation arose when rocket missiles under Moscow's control were set up on the island of Cuba, where the communist government of Fidel Castro had taken power (see p. 6, Photo 7). The missiles based so close to the U.S.A. at that time brought the two rival powers almost to the brink of war, and the situation was saved only when the U.S.S.R. withdrew. The U.S.A. has large military forces in many countries, and has formed military alliances, such as the North Atlantic Treaty Organization (NATO) with Britain, West Germany, Greece, Turkey, and other European countries. This treaty involves the stationing of American forces and bases in most of these countries, especially those which are not very strong. The South East Asia Treaty Organization (SEATO), involving Thailand, Australia, New Zealand, and the Philippines among

Photo. 158 The Aswan Dam

Photo. 159 American-backed Cuban invaders captured during the Bay of Pigs incident

133

Photo. 160 A U.S. Air Force helicopter drops soldiers in enemy-held territory in South Vietnam. The Americans supported the South in their fight against the communist North

others, is a similar alliance against communism in the Pacific Ocean area.

In the Eastern European communist interest, the Warsaw Pact binds together Poland, Czechoslovakia, Hungary and other countries. Soviet control is very strong. Although each country has its own elected (communist) government, and is free to make some decisions of a local kind, Moscow keeps a very close watch, and at times has used her huge military power to re-establish control. Soviet troops were used in Hungary and East Germany (German Democratic Republic) during the 1950's to crush rebellions against the governments of those countries; many Hungarian refugees fled to the West at that time. In Czechoslovakia in August 1968, troops from the U.S.S.R. moved in to take control and depose the Czech government, and again there was fighting in the streets.

The U.S.A., as a democratic power, has rarely interfered so brutally in the internal affairs of other countries. Cuba became a communist nation after Castro's successful revolution, and there was an attempt by the Americans, afterwards, to bring about the overthrow of Castro, by landing a group of anti-communist Cuban troops in the Bay of Pigs in 1961. However, the U.S. government did not try to stage a full invasion of Cuba, and the Bay of Pigs landing failed hopelessly. Previously, in 1953, when a communist government took control in the small Central American republic of Guatemala, and seized the large plantations of the American-owned United Fruit Company, support was given by the U.S.A. to a small invasion force which was able to overthrow the communists. Soon afterwards the plantations were returned to the United Fruit Company. Since then the U.S. government has supported the anti-communist regime; in 1960 American warships and aircraft were used to prevent a threatened invasion by communist forces.

China, apart from the border disputes with the U.S.S.R. (see p. 6 photo. 5), sent troops into Tibet in October 1950, and since then Tibet has been under Chinese rule. This high, mountainous country, very large in area but with very few people, was regarded by Chinese governments long before the communist revolution, as part of China, and the communists claimed in 1950 that they were merely taking over a part of their own country, although many Tibetans wished to be independent. Since the takeover, there has been further fighting in East Tibet between Chinese troops and Tibetan tribesmen, and disputes also, over the Indian border.

The Chinese government was not directly concerned when the war broke out in Korea in 1950, but when the American forces, acting under the United Nations flag, advanced as far as the border of China, the Peking government did send its army into North Korea against the Americans, and after the war ended in 1953 Chinese influence remained in North Korea just as American influence remains in the south.

The most obvious example of struggle between the great powers for control of other nations was the long and bitter war in Vietnam. In the south of Vietnam, an anti-communist government was at first aided by supplies of arms and advisers from America. Later, as the war grew, South Vietnam was directly supported by massive U.S. land, sea, and air forces against the communist government of the north which in turn was supplied with arms from the U.S.S.R., and supported by China. When the American troops were withdrawn, the northern forces soon conquered the south.

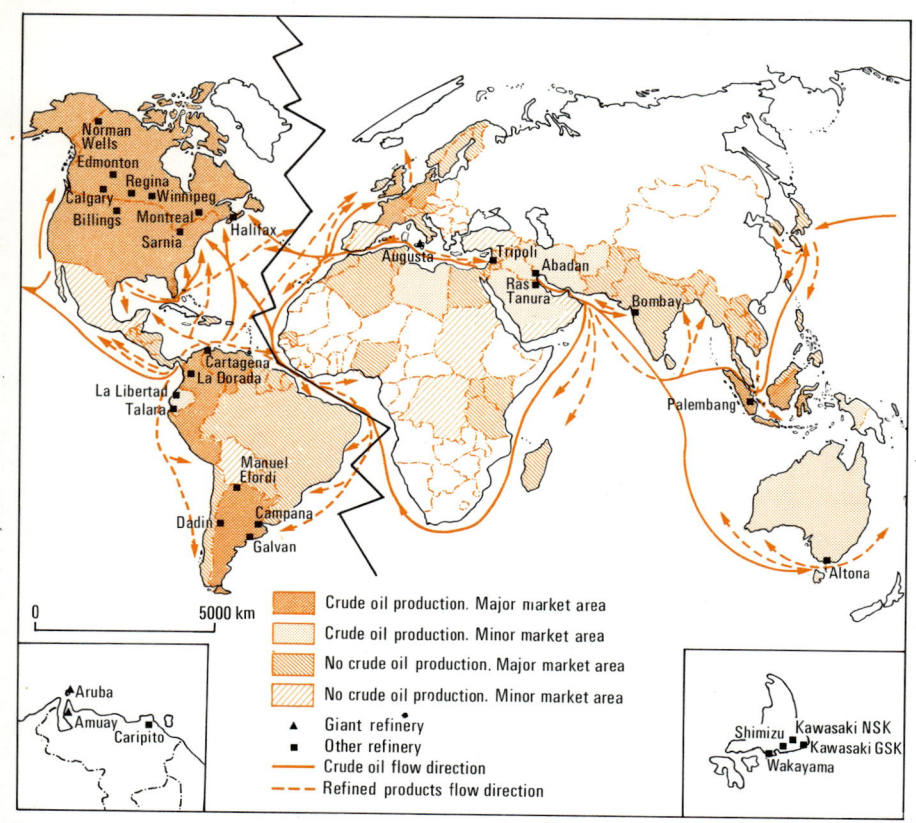

Fig. 53 A map prepared to show the countries supplying oil to one large American oil company, with the shipping routes used.

Influence by trade

Apart from actual warfare and domination by force, the great powers extend their influence through trade. This is particularly true of the U.S.A., since capitalism itself develops a system of trading which crosses oceans and frontiers. Consider the oil industry. As the oilfields in the U.S.A. run dry, new sources of oil are searched for overseas. The oil companies, which depend on the new finds, must make agreements with foreign governments both for the right to look for oil, and, when it is found, for the right to drill wells, build pipelines and refineries, and to ship the oil to the U.S.A. Some small, impoverished countries in the Middle East have great wealth in oil, and because of their agreements with American (and British) oil companies, and the dependence of the U.S.A. on such supplies, the American government supports and protects the governments with whom agreements have been made. Fig. 53 gives a list of countries providing oil to one huge American oil company (Standard Oil of New Jersey). Only a fraction of the oil comes from the U.S.A.

Small nations thus often see huge industries rising in their own countries, and many of them work for firms which are American-owned. This happens not only with oil, but with a great many other industries, in capitalist countries all over the world. The profits from the industry go mainly to shareholders in the U.S.A., though a certain proportion, by agreement, is paid to the local government. Such foreign-owned industries do contribute to the wealth of the country where they are situated, by providing jobs for the local people, training them in new skills, and sometimes providing housing and other social benefits.

China is probably too busy developing her own industries to be concerned with such outside interests, and the U.S.S.R. has so far not needed to import vital raw materials like oil, coal, or iron, since she has enough of her own. In recent times, however, both powers have increased trade with other countries. Wheat growers in Australia, Canada, and most recently, the U.S.A., have been able to sell large amounts of grain to both the U.S.S.R. and China. These capitalist countries once had a surplus of wheat and could not sell it all, so their farmers now want to increase trade with communist powers. Trade means not only the movement of goods and money from country to country, but also of people; contacts between trading countries develop, there are discussions and exchanges of ideas, personal friendships, and sometimes enmities, are formed. As long as trade continues, it pays both sides to work together to some extent. The more trade there is between the three giants themselves, the less the danger of war between them. Trade between giant powers and other nations, based on fair dealing and honest practices, is profitable to everyone.

Region and country	Gross	Net
Venezuela	1281.2	1063.9
Peru	36.1	34.9
Ecuador	1.3	1.2
Argentina	0.4	0.3
Colombia	0.2	0.2
Latin America	1 319.2	1 100.5
United States	**566.0**	**481.2**
Canada	111.1	97.4
Anglo-America	677.1	578.6
Saudi Arabia	417.8	417.8
Iraq	139.5	113.6
Iran	83.3	72.9
Libya	18.2	15.9
Middle East	658.8	620.2
France	29.9	27.0
Netherlands	19.3	19.3
Germany	4.0	4.0
Western Europe	53.2	50.3
Indonesia	35.6	35.6
West New Guinea (Irian)	0.6	0.6
South-East Asia	36.2	36.2
World Total	**2744.5**	**2385.8**

Assignments
1. Find out what you can about aid given to other countries by any of the three giant powers.
2. Find out which countries are members of NATO, SEATO, and the Warsaw Pact. Mark the countries concerned on the map. Are there any surprising gaps?
3. Locate on a world map the countries listed in Table 6 as supplying crude oil to the Standard Oil Company of New Jersey.
4. Search newspapers (especially business sections) for news of trade agreements between these powers.

Table 6 Countries supplying oil to Standard Oil of New Jersey, 1961. The figures show liquid production in thousands of barrels per day.

The Future...

All three giant powers are changing rapidly. It is difficult to predict what they will be like ten or twenty years from now. To guess even further ahead is almost impossible, yet most people who read this book will find their lives very greatly influenced and possibly changed beyond recognition by developments in China, the U.S.S.R. and the U.S.A. Will the three grow more alike as time goes on, or will they become more and more different?

The physical features, mountains and rivers and the climate, will not change much. But all three giant powers have very large plans for improving their desert lands. If these schemes succeed they will be followed by others and there is likely to be a gradual increase in the population of the arid areas.

The population of all the giant nations is increasing, China growing considerably more rapidly than the other two. If China continues to increase at the present rate for another twenty years the population will be 1000 million. Can such an increase actually take place? To feed such numbers, China would either have to increase her own food production enormously, or buy food from other countries. If the popula-

Photo. 161   Cooked meats for sale in Shanghai. Why do the assistants wear masks?

Photo. 162   Shopping in Moscow's Central Market

Photo. 163 Shops, hotels, and theatres in Las Vegas advertise their attractions. Note the heavy traffic

Photo. 164 Seafood at the Fishermen's Wharf in San Francisco. Other shopping scenes are shown in Photos. 39–42

tion can be fed, there will still be vast problems of housing, schooling, hospitals and other services.

A hundred years of such growth would fill the whole land area of China with dense population, even the mountainous regions would become as crowded as the Yangtze valley is already. Such a state of affairs is almost impossible to imagine and it seems certain that China's population growth will have to be controlled.

The U.S.S.R. has much more land area than China, fewer people, and a slower growth rate. But much of the land area is in the bitterly cold Siberian north, and crowding of the best land is increasing. In the U.S.A. the population is growing at a fairly slow but steady rate. Most American families have only two or three children. In the U.S.A., large families were common at one time, but as the country developed the fashion changed towards the smaller family. In China the government already encourages young people to marry late, which itself tends to reduce the number of children. Birth control is also encouraged.

Industries in the U.S.A. are well developed; in the U.S.S.R. they are

Photo. 165 Students at the University of Chicago

Photo. 167 Chinese students learn trade skills by making their own school equipment. Photos. 4 and 75 show younger children at school

Photo. 166 Before a lecture at Tashkent University, U.S.S.R.

Photo. 168 Students in a dormitory at the University of of Kunming

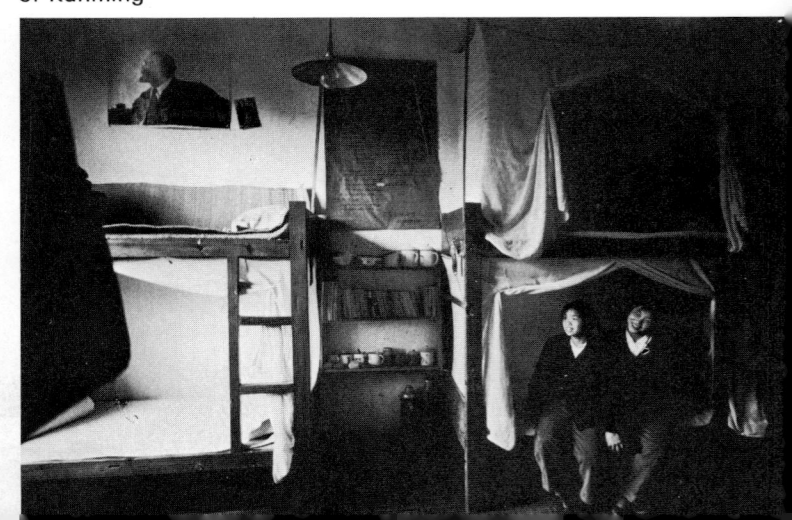

Photo. 169 Travelling to work on the Moscow underground

Photo. 170 Chinese children walk to a nearby kindergarten, each holding tight to the one in front. The tram takes their parents to work

developing rapidly, and in China they are going ahead with great speed. The processes involved, making steel, refining oil, building vehicles, are the same anywhere, but while the U.S.A. allows industry to be developed mainly by free enterprise and the demands of customers in competing shops, the communist governments make long term plans and control the factories directly, so there is often a good deal of difference in the way things are done. The communist powers needed first to build up their heavy industries—mining, transport, steel production, engineering—because without these, other industries cannot begin. Once these essential works are established, resources become available for light industries; making such things as refrigerators, electrical goods, radios, washing machines, cars, and fashionable clothing. Developments in the U.S.S.R. suggest that industry there will grow along similar lines to the U.S.A. China, where even heavy industry is still at a very early stage, may eventually follow the same pattern. At present, China's main concern is modernizing farming methods on the communes. Factories concentrate on making farm

Photo. 171   Many Chinese village families eat outside when the weather is warm

Photo. 172   Cossacks from the Rostov region in the U.S.S.R.

Photo. 173   An American family at home. Not all black Americans are poor

machinery, tractors, ploughs, harrows, seed drills, and on chemical fertilizers. Transport and the building of power stations, controlling the rivers to prevent flooding, and major projects of this kind, all have a high priority, so it is likely to be many years before China can turn attention to providing luxury goods for the people.

Capitalism and communism are both changing. Chinese communism is already different in many details from the Moscow variety, and while these differences may increase to some extent, political changes need not force the giants further apart. None have anything to gain by a major war, and all could benefit from further trade agreements and co-operation.

Photo. 175 Snowball battle in Moscow

Photo. 177 A group of Americans have afternoon tea at a hotel with a view across the San Francisco bay.

Photo. 174 Chess players in Gorki Park, Moscow

Photo. 176 This Chinese family enjoys a visit to a public park

Index

Alabama, 95
Alfalfa, 83
American Indians, 62
Anshan, 89, 94, 126
Area, 12
Arizona, 63
Armenians, 60
Arms race, 9
Arts, the, 115
Aswan Dam, 132
Atbasar, 79
Barley, 80–1
Black Sea, 49
Boston, 63
Budenny Collective, 78–9
California, 48, 63
Canton, 51–2, 56, 72–5, 118
Capitol, 116
Cattle, 77–8
Chelvata River, 79
Chicago, 95
China,
   Autonomous regions, 38
   Buddhists, 57
   Cultural Revolution, 24–5
   Farming, 141
   Government, 24–6
   Great Leap Forward, 90–1
   Industry, 91
   Moslems, 57
   Neighbourhood factories, 94
   Women, 94
Civil servants, 113
Coal-mining, 96–7
Collective farms, 78–9
Communes, 70, 72–5
Communications, 115
Company farms, 69, 82–5
Confucius, 57
Co-operative farms, 69
Cotton, 71, 83–4, 108
Crops, 86
Cuba, 126, 134
Democracy, 18, 134
Detroit, 105
Discrimination, 66

Donbass, 98
Education, 4–5, 73
Eskimos, 62
Federations, 37–8
Fishing, 73
Five Year Plans, 21, 29
Florida, 63
Foreign embassies, 113
Fruit crops, 72
Georgians, 60
Ghettos, 64
Gobi Desert, 42
Gorki, 78, 98, 106
Great Lakes, 118, 125
Han people, 54–5
Himalayas, 46
Ideograph, 56
Industry, 139—43
   Heavy, medium, light, 88
   Power for, 89
   Service industries, 89
   Centre of, 121
Karakoram Range, 46
Kazakhs, 58
Kharkov, 59
Kiev, 60
Korea, 135
Koreans, 58
Kostroma, 78–9
Kremlin, 116
Kuznetsk, 125
Labour-intensive, 86
Lenin, Nikolay, 23, 26
Leningrad, 118
Linen, 78–9
London, 111–12
Los Angeles, 63
Louisiana, 63
Lucerne mine, 95
Magnitogorsk, 79, 98, 111
Mandarin, 55
Manhattan, 108–9, 123
Mao Tse-tung, 24, 55
Marx, Karl, 26
Miami, 50–2
Middle East, 136

Minority groups, 66
Mississippi River, 62–3, 85
Mongols, 59
Monopolies, 33
Monsoon, 52, 72
Montana, 80–1
Monuments, national, 115
Moscow, 52, 98, 196, 112
Mount Everest, 46
Multi-cropping, 72
Nan Shan Range, 46
National security services, 113
NATO, 132
New Orleans, 63
New York, 63, 118, 123
Oil, 101–3, 136
Omsk, 50–2
Oxbows, 79
Pamirs, 46
Paotow, 94
Peking, 52, 56, 107, 112, 126
Permafrost, 45
Pennsylvania, 96, 97, 101
Pig-keeping, 73
Pittsburg, 95, 124–5
Pollution, 132
Population density, 13, 16, 138
Press, the (media), 20–2
Production brigade, 7, 77
Red Guard, 24
Rice, 73–5
Rocky Mountains, 46
Sacramento, 48, 63
St. Louis, 63
San Francisco, 63
Satellites, 9, 132
SEATO, 132
Shanghai, 118, 123, 127
Shensi, 76–7
Shenyang, 107, 124, 126
Sian, 76
Siberia, 139
Si-Kiang, 72
Sierra Nevada ranges, 46
Sinjao Commune, 72–3
Snow, 44

Socialism, 26
Soils,
   Loess, 76
   Black earth, 79
Soya beans, 82–3
Space exploration, 10
State farms, 69, 79
State ownership, 33
Steel, 91–5, 98–9, 124–6
Supreme Soviet, 38
Sverdlovsk, 79, 99, 124, 125, 126
Tanzania, 132
Temperatures, average, 50
Texas, 101
Textile industry, 108–9
Tibet, 57, 135
Trade, 137
   Centres of, 118
Trade unions, 32, 113
Ukraine, the, 60
Ural Mountains, 46, 98
United States of America
   Black (Afro-American) population, 64, 66
   Free enterprise, 28
   Government, 37
   President, 37
Union of Soviet Socialist
   Republics,
   Deserts, 42
   Government, 38
   Republics, 38
   1917 Revolution, 23
Vegetables, 77
Vehicle industry, 104
Vietnam, 132
Volga River, 78
Wall Street, 121
Warsaw Pact, 134
Washington, 52, 112, 123, 127
Wealth, 15
Wheat, 72, 77, 78, 79, 80–1, 86, 137
Wuhan, 91–2, 118
Yangtze River, 118, 139
Yuma, Arizona, 41